15 SCHOOL QUESTIONS AND DISCUSSION

From Class Size, Standards, and School Safety to Leadership and More

Mark F. Goldberg

A SCARECROWEDUCATION BOOK

The Scarecrow Press, Inc.
Lanham, Maryland, and Oxford
2002

A SCARECROWEDUCATION BOOK

Published in the United States of America
by Scarecrow Press, Inc.
A Member of the Rowman & Littlefield Publishing Group
4720 Boston Way, Lanham, Maryland 20706
www.scarecroweducation.com

PO Box 317
Oxford
OX2 9RU, UK

British Library Cataloguing in Publication Information Available

Library of Congress Cataloging-in-Publication Data

Goldberg, Mark F., 1938–
    15 school questions and discussion : from class size, standards, and school safety to
leadership and more / Mark F. Goldberg
        p. cm.
Includes bibliographical references and index.
    ISBN 0-8108-4356-0 (alk. paper)—ISBN 0-8108-4357-9 (pbk. : alk. paper)
    1. Education—United States—Handbooks, manuals, etc. 2. Teaching—United States—
Handbooks, manuals, etc. 3. Education—United States—Curricula—Handbooks,
manuals, etc. 4. School management and organization—United States—Handbooks,
manuals, etc. I. Title: Fifteen school questions and discussion. II. Title.
    LA209.2.G599 2002
    370'.973—dc21

                                                                        2002005859

♾™ The paper used in this publication meets the minimum requirements of
American National Standard for Information Sciences—Permanence of Paper for
Printed Library Materials, ANSI/NISO Z39.48-1992.
Manufactured in the United States of America.

CONTENTS

PART II   ALTERNATIVES TO TRADITIONAL
PUBLIC AND PRIVATE EDUCATION: VOUCHERS,
CHARTER SCHOOLS, AND HOME SCHOOLING

PART III   TEACHING AND LEARNING:
EIGHT INNOVATIONS

PART IV   LARGE ISSUES: SAFETY, LEADERSHIP,
AND QUALITY TEACHERS

FOREWORD

Over the past decade, education has become a highly politicized and, therefore, a highly complex, almost dizzying, endeavor. In defining their visions for America, both Bill Clinton and George W. Bush have dubbed themselves the "Education President," signaling how prominent education has become on the American landscape.

Many factors have contributed to the ascendancy of education's place in America's psyche. Among them:

- sweeping legislation passed by Congress and signed by President Bush that mandates annual reading and math testing in every state, grades 3–8;
- strong national support for the standards movement;
- research confirming that class sizes affect student learning;
- concerns about equity and achievement in schools, particularly for minority and Limited English Proficient students;
- questions about how to deal with "failing" schools, including the hotly debated role of school vouchers, charter schools, and home schooling; and
- growing fears about school safety.

Of slightly less importance in the national discussions about education, but still of paramount consequence within the field, are issues that directly affect the dynamics of teaching and learning. These issues include differentiated instruction, multiple intelligence theory, problem-based learning, and performance assessment.

In this well-written and sensible book, Mark Goldberg has captured virtually all of the issues, both political and educational, that are at the center of today's discussions about schooling. And, he has done it in an easily readable fashion by structuring the book around fifteen essential questions.

Dr. Goldberg takes the reader on a well-planned, highly structured journey through today's important issues, clarifying terms and concepts at each crucial milepost, and laying out opposing arguments in key debates.

The reader of this book not only will become more familiar with the important issues in education, but also with how they relate to one another. Dr. Goldberg helps us to understand the essence of each topic, and their interconnectedness. For example, the book draws associations between performance assessments and rubrics, content-rich curriculum and constructivist classrooms, class size and student performance, standards and accountability.

In addition to everything else, this book contains another juicy nugget—a section on leadership. Dr. Goldberg spent many years interviewing some of our nation's most prominent educational figures (Ernest Boyer, Seymour Papert, Madeline Hunter, Shirley Brice Heath, Theodore Sizer, and Deborah Meier to name a few), as well as two mayors who have played significant roles in their city's educational affairs (Kurt Schmoke of Baltimore and Rudolph Giuliani of New York). He analyzed their careers and shared his findings in a book, *Profiles of Leadership in Education*, Phi Delta Kappa Educational Foundation, 2000. The reader of this book will happily find a brief synopsis of his important findings.

Today, more than ever before, every citizen needs to have a basic understanding of the critical issues involved in education. This book provides that understanding in a clear, comprehensible, and very enjoyable manner.

> Martin G. Brooks, Ed.D.
> Superintendent of Schools, Plainview—Old Bethpage, N.Y.
> February 2002

PREFACE

No one should assume that his or her understanding of problem-based learning or constructivism or content-rich curriculum or standards is the correct one—even if that person wrote a book on the subject. Every issue and practice presented in this book is discussed, debated, revered or reviled, and used in some incarnation in school districts in many states—and in several cases in all states. There is no single accepted definition, custom, routine, method of operation, or system for school safety or educational leadership or testing or multiple intelligences or bilingual education or any other important and complex educational practice or concern—other than the many overlapping ways in which individual schools and districts adapt them.

I came to understand or be curious about the questions raised in this book in various ways. For instance, when interviewing Mayor Rudolph Giuliani of New York City or Hugh Price, President of the National Urban League, for a profile in The Phi Delta *Kappan*, such issues as standards, testing, and alternatives to failing schools came up. This happened again and again with a variety of subjects as I interviewed people for articles in the *Kappan* or *Educational Leadership*. Principals Dennis Littky and Debby Meier had their views and subjects; the late Albert Shanker, Harold Hodginson, John Goodlad, Carol Gilligan, Governor

Lowell Weicker, English teacher Florence Mondry, and many other people I interviewed for an article had special questions, attitudes, and favorite programs or methods.

I have served as development editor for more than thirty books published by Association for Supervision and Curriculum Development (ASCD) and Corwin Press since 1995. Working with Ann Lambros on problem-based learning, Timm Mackley on content-rich curriculum, Giselle Martin-Kniep on teacher portfolios, Linda Campbell on multiple intelligences, and many other experts on so many topics acquainted me with the whole field of an author's interest. When working with authors, I am drawn to conferences, articles, other books, and Internet information on their topics. Each author has a strong point of view, but the other points of view on their chosen subject also became known to me. Of course, much information on the advisory system in secondary schools or leadership can be traced directly back to me. I wrote one small book on the advisory system and two slightly longer books on leadership.

I take full responsibility for everything in this book. In the end, the point of view and selection of examples are mine. I am indebted, to be sure, to hundreds of people who have invited me to their classrooms and schools, who have spoken or written about the subjects in this book, or who are in the news occasionally holding forth on some of these subjects. Again, I determined what to include and how to present it.

ACKNOWLEDGMENTS

After a very long and remarkably successful college teaching career, my greatest teacher, Professor Joseph Locke Slater, died on February 22, 2001.

Dr. Slater had many gifts in the classroom. He brought an enormous command of American literature and a particular love for the literature of the nineteenth century to his students. Professor Slater lectured, encouraged students to speak and ask questions, often asked a student he knew to have special expertise in, for instance, a foreign language or religion to clarify a point, asked his students to write on topics that were original, honored his students when they made helpful or incisive comments, but never embarrassed a student who struggled to keep up with Joe Slater's very high standards for how a class should be conducted.

Outside of class, Professor Slater often held conversations with small groups of students in or near his English department office and encouraged individual visits to talk about literature or other concerns. In my senior year, I was the college newspaper's theater reviewer for New York plays. More often than not, I either received a short note or a comment after class about my latest review.

Slater expected his students to read literature with great care and to care deeply about what they read. He assumed his students would want to read literary criticism and biography to learn more about the great writers he so admired—but only after they had first worked hard to appreciate the writer in his or her own words. Emerson, Thoreau, Dickinson, Melville, Hawthorne, Whitman, Twain and James were the eight American writers Slater cherished most.

Professor Slater saw literature as a vital and necessary part of the educated life. Students rarely missed one of his classes. In the winter, one heard sneezes and coughs in the room, but no seats were empty. I don't think I ever missed or was even late for a Slater class. He loved language and used it very precisely. Once I took the young woman who was to become my wife to his office to meet him. She sat in a chair that suddenly slipped back a few inches. Professor Slater immediately reassured us, "It's treacherous but not deadly."

How lucky I was to experience this very great teacher in several classes and to come to know him a bit outside of the classroom. A member of the extraordinary generation that endured the Great Depression and then went off to fight a war, Joseph Locke Slater came back to pass on his undisturbed enthusiasm for fine literature, for intellectual excellence, and for life in general to thousands of fortunate students at my alma mater Rutgers University and after that at his alma mater Colgate University.

INTRODUCTION

Since Sputnik was placed in space by the then–Soviet Union in October 1957, American education has undergone constant and sometimes turbulent change. At first, the changes were in curriculum, particularly in the sciences (Biological Sciences Curriculum Study—BSSC; Physical Science Study Committee—PSSC). Soon after, John Holt (*How Children Fail*, Dell Publishing Co., 1964) told us that no curriculum works well unless the students are allowed to follow their own natural curiosity. In 1967, Jonathan Kozol published *Death at an Early Age* (Houghton Mifflin), detailing the utter failure of Boston's inner-city schools—and by extension the inner city schools of, perhaps, two dozen other metropolises in the United States. From the late 1950s to 1982, three of the principal issues that would continue for the remainder of the century and into the twenty-first century were clear, although the categories and complexities under each principal issue have expanded:

- Curriculum—What should we teach, and how should we assess what we teach? What methods should we use in our teaching?
- Learning—How do young people learn? Do we emphasize process or content? What do we know that can guide us? What are some new developments that hold great promise?

- Equity in All of Its Forms—How do we provide a level playing field
  for the millions of poor and minority children whose school districts and families do not have the resources to provide the advantages that benefit middle and upper-middle class children? What
  resources or methods will be required to improve the schools in
  disadvantaged areas—to turn them into safe places where sound
  instruction takes place?

In the years since 1982, and particularly since 1983 when "A Nation at
Risk" warned us that some of our schools were becoming mediocre, educators have researched and experimented with new methods, techniques,
and curriculum approaches in an effort to make our schools better. From
action research and content-rich curriculum to multiple intelligences, from
debates about standards, assessment, and class size to problem-based
learning, constructivism, and safety, American schools have been bom-
barded with a bewildering array of choices and mandates, some of them
quite sound and rooted in theory, research, and practice and others largely
politically motivated or based on inadequate research and experience.

Educators have continued to wrestle with the problem of equity, used in
the broadest sense possible, in new ways—even, sadly, in the past ten years
adding the issue of physical safety in schools to the mix. For years, violence
in schools has been associated with schools in poor city neighborhoods. We
now see occasionally some angry, depressed young person goes on a ram-
page and injures or kills people, making some middle-class schools far less
safe than any inner-city school. The equity issue—taken very broadly to include school finance, quality of education, and safety—has spun off a
fourth major issue for our time: How much choice should be allowed in
schooling? Should parents be able to send their children to any school of
their choice or even keep their children at home for their education? How
can this work? What role should physical safety play in choice? How can
parents judge whether a school is safe?

Two indisputable facts have emerged from the work of the last forty-
five years that cut across all of the issues mentioned. First, school districts vary in what they need and in what the local community wants. For
instance, some communities desire a curriculum that emphasizes "important" information; others prefer an emphasis on "important" methods for learning and feel that information is not so crucial in our tech-

nological society. Of course, the word important could be debated into eternity. Second, some school districts have undeniable, non-debatable needs that vary enormously. If your reading scores, for instance, are considerably below grade level year after year, better approaches and interventions for helping students read well must be found. If your school has a problem with violent behavior, that must be addressed immediately and vigorously. If your brightest students are not in a demanding enough program and not gaining acceptance to competitive colleges, something new must be introduced.

Neither this book nor any other single book can present all of the information you need on the explosion of issues and programs out there, but this book attempts to be a good start. I decided that just listing one hundred or more program titles and methods and supplying a brief explanation would not serve my purpose. There are several education "dictionaries" available—not to mention the Internet. Ronald Brandt's 1997 book, *The Language of Learning: A Guide to Education Terms* (ASCD) is an example of a very helpful book for getting quick and accurate definitions of an education term or process.

What many educators and certainly the two million new educators who will enter the profession in the next ten years need, is a short (several pages) but serious and solidly grounded discussion of many of the issues or programs of greatest interest followed by some details and perspective. I have supplied explanations of 1,000 to 2,200 words for each question I raise, enough to help an administrator or teacher become reasonably conversant with the issue, to determine if she or he wants to know more, and to understand if this issue or program might be of consequence in that person's school or district. The bonus for readers is that they will begin to understand many of the dominating concerns of the education profession at the start of the twenty-first century.

This book is divided into four parts that get at the issues identified above:

- Part I—Curriculum Influences: Standards, Tests, and Class Size
- Part II—Alternatives to Traditional Public and Private School Education: Vouchers, Charters Schools, and Home Schooling
- Part III—Teaching and Learning: Eight Innovations
- Part IV—Large Issues: Safety, Leadership, and Quality Teachers

Each part has the same organization:

- Question—The question is posed.
- Discussion—Enough information is provided for the reader to understand just what is captured in the question. Sometimes a short paragraph is sufficient; in other cases, the basic discussion goes on for a full page or slightly more.
- Perspective and Details—This is the longest of the three parts in every case. In a few instances, answers or beginnings of answers or tentative answers are provided. More often, I simply provide enough information for the reader to understand in some detail just what is at stake here and what directions might be taken.

Following are some sample questions:

- What do I need to know about tests?
- What will be required to keep schools safe?
- What do I need to know about vouchers?
- What are differentiated instruction, problem-based learning, and multiple intelligences?
- What are some characteristics of leadership in education?

Again, not every question an educator could ask is covered in this book, but fifteen frequently debated questions of considerable importance and complexity are presented. Each of these questions is based on my perception that newspapers, magazines, serious TV talk shows, education journals, and conferences feature them; parents, politicians, and business leaders talk about most of them; educators come across these questions everywhere from teacher preparation courses to their classrooms and schools.

Of course, I selected the issues and programs to present as questions in this book, and without hesitation I admit that some of my biases are in the "answers"—neither unfairly nor blatantly, I hope. Also, experts in each of the areas might not agree with everything I say, although I tried faithfully to capture the meaning or argument or practice behind each question as it is played out in the educational community today. All of the questions I raise are on large and controversial areas in the field, so not every faction or interest group could possibly be happy with what I say. In fact, many of the questions I present have been subjected to highly emotional debates in educational, community, business, media, and political forums. My hope is that I have provided enough information and perspective to frame the debate and even supply some direction to the interested parties.

If this book is successful, I or someone else will do a similar book in a few years with somewhat different responses to the same questions or perhaps some additional questions of equal importance. Several of the same questions might be raised, but the discussion, perspective, and details may not be the same.

Ours is a complex and ever-changing profession. In the first two decades of my work in schools, there were no computers in the buildings and no one in my acquaintance spoke such words and phrases as "constructivism" or "problem-based learning" or "multiple intelligences." Now technology and such new programs as I just mentioned are heard at every large conference on education. We know much more about how to help children learn than we did in 1960, and I hope this book will help to place some of the large issues and recently developed forms of assistance before a new generation of teachers and administrators. I am confident that no one will ever write the definitive book that tells all educators what the "right" answers are to the large questions we must ask ourselves anew each few years. Our nation is too big and too varied for that, and what we know and need to know changes very rapidly.

I

CURRICULUM INFLUENCES:
STANDARDS, TESTS, AND CLASS SIZE

This part examines the following questions.

Question 1: What are standards, and what do I need to know about
   them?
Question 2: What do I need to know about tests?
Question 3: What are some of the issues around the country with the
   standards/testing movement?
Question 4: What do I need to know about class size?

You cannot visit a school, attend a conference, or talk to a school offi-
cial without having the issues of standards and tests come up—and frequently the issue of class size. Like it or not, standards and tests are part
of the national landscape, and they are not going away, although they are
undergoing continual change. There are federal, state, and local mandates. The standards/tests conversation takes place constantly in schools,
state education departments, in the media, at every political level, and
at the national and local meetings of the National Education Association
(NEA) and the American Federation of Teachers (AFT).

Standards and the tests that flow from them are now so much a part of
the landscape that the September 2001 issue of *Educational Leadership*

(EL) took as its theme "Making Standards Work." EL editor Marge Scherer in her "Perspectives" column stated that for the past decade, the journal "has often presented the debate for and against establishing standards. . . . Some of our authors have examined the dark side of overemphasized testing, and some authors have expressed concerns about misused tests" (p. 5). The September 2001 issue does not focus on the dark side but concentrates on how to make the best use of standards when reforming curriculum and creating useful assessments.

Class size is both a substantive and a political/budgetary discussion that concerns every board of education in the country. Do we need to reduce class size? If the answer is yes, that means training and hiring more teachers. If the answer is no, we are saying our current class sizes are ideal or close to it, or we cannot afford to do what is right. Then what?

These particular educational concerns, standards, tests, and class size have been in the news with some frequency for the past several years. Both Presidents Bush and Clinton made education and these issues part of the national discussion of education. Some people laud standards and tests as the answer to all of education's ills; others condemn their narrowness and unfairness. Some educators think, within reason, that class size makes little difference; others believe that it is one of a small number of very powerful determinants of student success. Of course, the issues and arguments are more complex than that, so following is a beginning effort to sort things out.

❶

WHAT ARE STANDARDS, AND WHAT DO I NEED TO KNOW ABOUT THEM?

DISCUSSION

In the past decade, forty-nine of the fifty states have constructed learning standards designed to tell teachers at each grade level what students should know and be able to do. Iowa, the lone holdout, has mandated that local districts do this rather than the state, but the state does use the Iowa Test of Basic Skills (ITBS) as one gauge for how students are progressing. Ostensibly, standards are a good idea. After all, if you know just what is expected, you can take steps to make things good happen. Unfortunately, standards are a bit more complicated than that.

Those in favor of standards say that having a set of clear and rigorous standards allows everyone to know just what is expected. Curriculum development becomes sounder because it is based on a known set of standards or objectives, dozens for each subject area, and many of those broken down into constituent elements. Appropriate materials and methods can be developed to help achieve the standards. Assessment completes the cycle. You test what is important—namely, the agreed-upon standards—and you know which schools need to be improved and which students need additional help. Since the standards are statewide, the tests can be developed rather carefully by a qualified committee at the state level or commercially developed tests can be purchased. These carefully developed tests for several subject areas, usually standardized and paper-and-pencil, can all be taken in the space of a few days and, for the most part, can be machine scored.

The anti-standards argument begins with determining just what is important. The only way to reach agreement is to form committees at the state level and then impose standards; otherwise, each school district or school will insist on its own notions of what is important. That means that teachers are told what to do rather than included in shaping the curriculum. The curriculum is somewhat limited because it is conditioned by the final assessment, created by a committee or testing company far removed from any individual school district, that determines who looks good and who does not. Since tests are expensive, everything will be based on a single test or set of tests, and those will be mostly multiple-choice or short answer. If we give many tests and ask students to write thoughtful essays or demonstrate competence in a science lab or apply their math to a real-world situation, it will be expensive and complicated to do assessment and some subjectivity will enter into the equation.

PERSPECTIVE AND DETAILS

There are many different types of standards, but most of them can be subsumed under three headings:

- Content Standards tell you what students need to learn: the stories they should read, the math they should do, the science they should learn or practice in a laboratory.
- Performance Standards tell you the acceptable level for determining that a student has mastered the material to at least the required minimum. Of course, if a student exceeds the minimum, all the better.
- Opportunity-to-Learn Standards set out the resources, conditions, and any other factors that will allow each student to have an equal chance to meet the state standards.

Educators all over the country have struggled with standards, and some states have done very good things, but the complications and difficulties remain because students and local conditions vary so much and because the ability to construct all the necessary and sufficient conditions for success vary so much. Judy F. Carr and Douglas E. Harris wrote a helpful book on standards (*Succeeding with Standards: Linking Curriculum, Assessment, and Action Planning*, ASCD, 2001). One has only to skim the book to understand that this is complicated stuff requiring a great deal of preparation.

The standards themselves are often derived from work done by national organizations and then adapted to state needs. The National Council of Teachers of Mathematics (NCTM) and The National Council of Teachers of English (NCTE), for instance, have documents on standards in their respective areas. Infrequently, the standards of a respected organization are just accepted, in many cases they are adapted or combined with existing objectives, goals, and mandates, and many states have created a few of their own local standards to reflect their idiosyncratic concerns. The point here is that there is no universally accepted national directory of "best standards," although there is considerable overlap among the states.

Once standards are determined, much work needs to be done. Carr and Harris talk about determining who is to teach each standard, creating a curriculum and assessment plan, defining effective practice, creating a comprehensive assessment system, and mapping out a path to success through action planning. This is reasonably clear, and their book makes it even clearer—supplying the details necessary to accomplish all of these things. So what could be the problem? Let's go back to the three types of standards and examine those to see where some issues exist.

Content Standards

Some children come from advantaged backgrounds and others from disadvantaged backgrounds. Since there are also variations among the abilities of children without regard to background, ethnicity, or anything else, what are the appropriate content standards for every child of every background, need, and ability? We want the disadvantaged children to make progress, so perhaps we should set the content standards very high. But won't some children be frustrated if the standards are beyond their reach at the time of instruction and testing? If we set the standards

6

too low, won't the brightest children, advantaged or not, be bored? Is it possible for any one set of standards or single curriculum to accommodate all children in states as complex as California or New York or Texas? Perhaps it is the children in every state who are too complex to fit into one system of standards?

Performance Standards

This is where we say exactly what a youngster should be able to do. The child should be able to perform these six math operations in grade 5, or the child should be able to read a short passage and respond in writing at, say, paragraph length to a question about that passage. Perhaps we've even created a rubric for determining if the paragraph is adequate. Here, of course, we run into the same questions that plagued us with content standards. What is the right level of performance? How do we consider all the complications of background and variations in ability among all children—or should we simply say here is the content, here is the performance standard, and here is how we'll help students master this? That leads us to opportunity standards.

Opportunity-to-Learn Standards

If taken seriously, opportunity standards mean that we have an obligation to do whatever is necessary to enable all children to have an equal chance to learn and to do well on assessments of their learning. The state has said "here are the standards, and let's be generous in our assumption of how they have been presented." The standards are clear; they've been broken down into the practical elements teachers can understand, and each teacher knows what she or he is expected to teach in a particular year under the standards program. In addition, the district has created a curriculum that is very strongly linked to the standards, there have been workshops on effective practice, and there is even a comprehensive plan for what teachers and schools can do to ensure that students master the material. The tests are very closely aligned to the standards and even include some elements of performance and exhibition.

It sounds as if these people have read the Carr and Harris book or if they're in the state of Washington, they've read Bruce and Linda

Campbell's very helpful book *Washington: A State of Learning* (Campbell and Assoc., Inc., 2000) which provides lots of background and gives teachers sample lessons for many of the standards. They've even gone somewhat beyond the recommendations of those authors.

But opportunity is far more complex than just that.

- Mary-1 is in a suburban school in Texas or Illinois or Arizona. There are nineteen students in her fifth-grade class. In the computer corner, there are three fairly new computers just for her class and an assortment of age-appropriate CD-ROMs or DVD-ROMs. Her teacher has tenure, a masters' degree, and is currently enrolled in both a college course and an inservice course for which she'll get salary credit. Her classroom is commodious, colorful, and filled with books, math and science materials, and plenty of supplies for projects. There is a paraprofessional who helps the children, particularly with reading and math, two days each week. Several parent volunteers, one or two of them college-educated and one a former teacher, come to the classroom at least twice each month on a regular schedule.
- Mary-2 is in an inner-city school, and there are twenty-six youngsters in her fifth-grade class. There is one fairly new computer in the classroom but only two or three CD-ROMs and no DVD-ROMs. Her teacher is inexperienced and too overwhelmed this year to take any courses. In fact, she's planning to leave at the end of the year. The room is slightly crowded, there are some books, but most materials are in short supply, particularly some of the more expensive science materials. The paraprofessional comes in for four hours each week to help the children with reading and math. There are one or two parent volunteers, but they are not college educated and due to other obligations cannot maintain a dependable schedule.

I think almost everyone would agree that Mary-1's opportunity standards give her some advantages.

Presenting any criticism of standards, however mildly or sensibly or constructively, when most Democrat and Republican lawmakers, including a strong majority of governors, favor them and even the American

Federation of Teachers supports standards is tantamount to criticizing motherhood and apple pie. When most people, particularly non-educators, hear the word standards, they think higher standards or tougher standards and better test scores. When many politicians hear the word standards, they think improving test scores that will help them get reelected. So educators must do two jobs. First, make the entire standards movement more sensible and equitable for all children. Second, educate the public about the complexity of standards.

The standards movement is not going away, and perhaps it should not go away, but there will be adjustments. There have been too many places where passing test scores have been raised or lowered, where standards have been adjusted, or where parents and educators have complained loudly to believe that this issue is settled. What is needed is for educators and the public to work together to find reasonable standards, to allow teachers to exercise their best judgment and creativity while preparing students to meet the standards, to make the tests more sophisticated and reflective of important learning, and to do whatever must be done to grant students who need help or time or resources to perform well to get those things. Without question, creating standards, and especially creating reasonably high standards, has forced many under-performing schools to face the fact that they have not been doing a good job educating children, particularly poor children. However, all of us must continue to look at and work with this movement for years to come to make it far sounder and better understood.

More information about standards and the issues and problems they raise will be provided in response to Question 3: What are some of the issues around the country with the standards/testing movement?

2

WHAT DO I NEED TO KNOW ABOUT TESTS?

DISCUSSION

There is no way around testing. Tests in American schools have been with us for at least one hundred years, and since the publication in 1983 of "A Nation at Risk," the demand for standards and accountability has been deafening. Of course, most of accountability is testing students at regular intervals. Teachers give classroom tests of all sorts, and large education testing corporations or state education departments supply standardized tests to schools that may have considerable impact on the future of a student or a school. In some cases, teachers and principals can even get rewards for good scores ranging from increased salaries or additional classroom materials to transfers to "more desirable" classes and schools.

Tests are neither inherently good nor bad, and most tests produced by large organizations are constructed rather carefully. On April 9, 2000, Jim Yardley published a long piece in the Education Life section of the Sunday *New York Times* on how the Psychological Corporation of San Antonio goes about the painstaking process of making new versions of the Stanford Achievement Test. The tests are made in great secrecy behind a chain-link fence, and care is exercised to make the tests as fair as possible. Even then, errors are made in question construction and scoring, but far more often than not the tests are sound—meaning they do what they were intended to do.

PERSPECTIVE AND DETAILS

So why the hue and cry over such tests as the Iowa Test of Basic Skills, the Stanford Achievement Test, and so many of the new tests constructed by individual states to measure their particular standards?

It is devilishly difficult to make a fair test, no matter how much effort is expended. The moment you use a word or phrase that is more familiar to a rural or urban or African-American or Italian-American student, you are in trouble. When you use such phrases as "subdivision" or "mosque" or "block-and-tackle" or "bodega" or "subway" or "combine," you skew the test in favor of some category of students and leave another group somewhat mystified. You end up with tests, after considerable field testing and tweaking, that are rather bland, but soon enough and inevitably you learn that the test was indeed unfair to some group. Of course, no one has yet figured out how to make tests fair when one student comes from a disadvantaged home and another from an advantaged home, when some students come from a farm community and others from a very large city, or when some students have a background that emphasizes deep knowledge of a particular religion and others come from a much more secular background.

Students whose families read books, newspapers, and magazines, watch educational television, travel, speak standard English, and provide a computer, lots of supplies, and a quiet place for study will always have a built-in advantage on paper and pencil tests and most other tests of any kind.

Most of the large-group tests are multiple choice or short answer. Too often, teachers focus on the information they know or anticipate will be on the test and find little time for richer classroom experiences. Professor Linda McNeil, Professor of Education and Director of the Center for Education at Rice University, is a critic of the standardized state tests given in Texas (Texas Assessment of Academic Skills—TAAS). She is quoted in an article by Michael Sadowski ("Harvard Education Letter:

Research Online," September/October 2000) as saying that the tests distort classroom instruction. There are classrooms in Texas, according to McNeil, where "children read no prose from September to February." They read only very short passages similar to what they will find on the TAAS. In McNeil's words, "They study information they are meant to forget. It's all artificial content to raise test scores" (p. 4). In fairness, Texas is making some changes in their required tests over the next few years and is even changing the name from TAAS to TAKS (Texas Assessment of Knowledge and Skills). It remains to be seen if Linda McNeil's criticism will continue to apply at all or to what extent.

Classroom teachers emphasize what will be tested and reduce emphasis on what will not be tested. In spite of protests from administrators and politicians that there is ample time for sophisticated units on government or the environment or local issues, teachers everywhere say it just isn't so. Many standardized tests produced by commercial publishers do not match state standards or curriculum. Even worse, many of a state's own tests are not aligned with the state's own standards, so the curriculum as actually practiced by teachers is out of whack. All or parts of a standard or curriculum may be eliminated from a test because the item is too common, too easy. Test items are assigned a p-value that represents the percentage of students who answer an item correctly. "An item with a p-value of .85 would have been answered correctly by 85 percent of those who attempted to answer it. A test item correctly answered by exactly half of the examinees would have a p-value of .50" (*The Truth about Testing: An Educator's Call to Action*, W. James Popham, ASCD, 2001, p. 47). Items that represent important standards and are included in the curriculum but that many students answer correctly are soon removed from the test because they don't discriminate among students. As soon as teachers understand this, they stop teaching that part of the curriculum, emphasize things that will be on the test, and the standards, curriculum, actual teaching, and assessment quickly get out of alignment.

Common sense should tell us that a single test or very limited set of tests—especially if the test has serious consequences for students, staff, and schools—is patently unfair. Question 3 will cover this in more detail. However, it should be clear that no test is even close to perfect, individual students have "bad" days that do not represent their true ability, some able students are poor test takers and even feel ill when faced with a high-stakes test, and some students of good ability just do not take the tests seriously. Most tests are limited to multiple choice, short answer, or other restricted and delimited methods of assessment of a student's ability. No one test or set of tests, therefore, is a complete or accurate assessment of a student's accomplishment, and occasionally the test is a very poor reflection of a student's work. Is there any reader of this book who does not know several people who perform very well in school or at work, but do not get "test" or "performance" scores that reflect that good work?

Giving high-stakes tests every year is a prescription for educational and political disaster. Most of our nation's elementary schools are small— thousands of schools with fewer than six hundred students in grades K–5 or K–6. In a given year, a small number of unusually bright students or poor test takers or poorly behaved students or students whose parents choose not to send them to school on test day because they are "ill" or some other small category of students in one grade can wittingly or un- wittingly skew the results for their grade. A grade or school that is not do- ing an excellent job might look better than it should. A school that is doing a good job will normally show excellent results over several years, but will have an occasional year when little obvious progress is made. That school will be roundly criticized by local administrators and politi- cians for a year, you can be sure, even though what is happening is com- pletely normal in the trajectory of a school doing good work. This will certainly affect the morale of a staff that is working hard and well.

The only way to know if a student can write a careful essay or conduct a serious science lab process or respond to questions about an interest- ing math problem or draw reasonable inferences from historical data or do anything else worth assessing is to ask that student to do those things several times. Early student efforts should be used for training and di- agnosis, and it should be the pattern of a student's work over time, per- haps months, that is accepted as an accurate reflection of that individ- ual's accomplishment.

Generally speaking, classroom teachers do not like single high-stakes tests. In the summer 2001 meeting of the National Education Associa- tion (NEA), the nation's largest teacher group, this was a hot topic that came up several times. The NEA does not oppose the use of standard- ized tests "in combination with other assessment tools, such as teacher evaluations and educator-derived quizzes. But the organization categorically opposes the use of tests as the sole criterion for promoting students to the next grade, awarding high school diplomas, and rewarding or penalizing schools" ("Education Week on the Web," July 11, 2001, p. 1). Some of the criticisms leveled at the high-stakes tests include that they limit curriculum richness, reduce teacher creativity and student joy in learning, drive some of the most talented and creative teachers from the profession, and sometimes make students physically and emotionally ill.

Adjustments have been made and continue to be made in most state testing programs. However, it remains a healthy view to look at the tests and the results each year with a wary eye and with the attitude that we want them to become better. This is not a criticism of the honest effort most states have made to get it right within the existing political and budget constraints. It is simply recognition of how difficult it is to create tests that are fair, challenging, interesting to young people, and truly reflective of the important standards many states have created.

WHAT ARE SOME OF THE ISSUES AROUND THE COUNTRY WITH THE STANDARDS/TESTING MOVEMENT?

DISCUSSION

Questions 1 and 2 examined standards and tests separately. This question looks at some of the problems that the standards/testing movement has embedded within it or has encountered from constituents who are not entirely satisfied with the movement.

While standards and tests have been around in many forms since the 1880s, only recently have many states and cities adopted "high-stakes testing." The stakes are high because schools may gain or lose funding based on test results, students may or may not be promoted, teachers and principals may or may not get bonuses, be shifted to other schools, or even get fired. In other words, high-stakes testing can lead to real-world consequences.

Standards are intended to provide the basis for instruction, assessment establishes benchmarks for schools to achieve, and the assessment results ostensibly allow the professional staff to figure out who is learning and who is not. If the standards are sophisticated and properly high, if the curriculum is aligned with the standards, and if the assessment accurately and faithfully tests the standards, everything should work.

PERSPECTIVE AND DETAILS

Well, everything is not working. Without question, some states have suc-
ceeded in making the curriculum more rigorous and sounding a call to
underperforming schools that persistently and pervasively poor results
will not be tolerated, but the standards and testing movement, still in a
very early stage, has many problems, inevitable in a complex undertak-
ing where much is at stake for students, school faculties, parents, education officials, and politicians. Parents, teachers, teacher organizations,
local, state and federal politicians, special interest groups, consultants,
and others all have a strong opinion about the standards/testing movement, and those opinions vary greatly. Following are some of the concerns each constituency must consider.

That most tests are given once and on a particular day or week of
the year has already been mentioned. As former Secretary of Education Richard Riley has said, "If all of our efforts to raise standards get
reduced to one test, we've gotten it wrong" (ASCD, "Infobrief," November 2000, p. 3). How many of us would like to be judged for high
stakes on the basis of one day or one test? Randy Johnson and Tiger
Woods have bad days; their income and status are based on at least a
year or a season, not a particular day.

A serious criticism of many of the new tests, especially limited tests
with multiple choice and short answer sections, is that kids are not learning much new information—only how to take that particular test. In an
Op-Ed piece in the *New York Times* on December 4, 1998, Howard
Gardner, a professor at the Harvard Graduate School of Education,
wrote about the new tests in the Chicago schools "that whenever a new
test was adopted, scores immediately dropped" (p. 31). After a few
years, scores recovered "as students and teachers became accustomed to
the test" (p. 31). The evidence points to the probability that a limited
number of test items and familiarity with the format cause scores to rise
rather than increased learning of important information.

We say that we want students to write well, to think critically, to find
creative solutions to problems, to work well in groups, and to do other
important things that our culture values. However, these things are
rarely tested on the new state tests. In a January 12, 2001 article summarizing a teacher survey in "Education Week on the Web," it was re-

ported that "Sixty-six percent said state tests were forcing them to con-centrate too much on what's tested to the detriment of other important topics" (p. 3). Teachers around the country are dropping multi-week projects that focused on critical thinking or problem solving in favor of getting students ready for the big test of, largely, information. As Gerald W. Bracey said in the October 2001 issue of the Phi Delta *Kappan*, we should consider some of the important things that most standardized tests do not measure: "creativity, critical thinking, resilience, motivation, persistence, humor, reliability, enthusiasm, civic-mindedness, empathy, leadership, and compassion" ("The 11th Bracey Report on the Condi-tion of Public Education," p. 158). The October issue came out just af-ter the devastating attack on America, but the article was obviously com-pleted months before publication date. Virtually every quality Bracey mentioned has turned out to be crucial for politicians and our military forces in the aftermath of the attack—but, again, these very important qualities are not ones we usually test, and that means teachers won't spend very much of their limited time on them.

Far too often, the tests are for gatekeeping purposes rather than di-agnosis. We say this or that student gets promoted or this teacher is not doing well. The more important purposes of the tests would be to de-termine what an individual child is learning or not learning or where the teacher or school are deficient—and then to take some reasonable and important pedagogical action based on those findings. There is too much talk about taking punitive action if a school's scores are poor for a stated period of time and not enough talk about taking constructive steps every year to bring about improvement.

If students are going to be subjected to high-stakes testing, the prepa-ration system must be fair. We cannot change the socio-economic status of students very easily or quickly, but we certainly should make the school experience of poor students more nearly equal to that of students in more affluent communities. This was discussed in Question 1 in the Mary-1 and Mary-2 examples. It remains the case that advantaged students generally do better on tests than disadvantaged students. Changing parents' education or income is very difficult; improving schools, no piece of cake, can be done and will make a difference. Until under-performing schools, often in cities, are brought up to a higher standard—usually that of the middle class suburban schools—there will be efforts such as the one in Memphis, Tennessee, to lower the passing score for that city. State school board member Avron Fogelman announced he would "propose that the board set up lower performance standards for Memphis than the rest of Tennessee. He believes you just can't compare an urban district plagued with poverty to other school districts in the state" (Aimee Edmondson, "The Commercial Appeal," November 16, 2001—www.gomemphis.com/mca/local_news/article, p. 1).

Parents and school districts around the country are protesting that the tests are not fair, not relevant to the students in that district, or downright harmful. In Scarsdale, New York, a very affluent town, several hundred parents protested that the state tests were reducing the rigor and quality of the curriculum, and many of those parents kept their children home in spring 2001 when tests were given. Scarsdale administers more demanding tests than the state as well as identifies students having difficulty and provides those students with considerable help. When Dr. Richard P. Mills was education commissioner in Vermont, he favored portfolios to measure achievement and condemned single test scores. Now commissioner in New York, when asked if the state tests might be "purposeless for Scarsdale, Dr. Mills said, "I can't ignore what they did. We're looking for uniformity" (*New York Times*, November 18, 2001, A27, Michael Winerip).

Advocates for vocational students in Massachusetts believe the Massachusetts Comprehensive Assessment System (MCAS) test has very little to do with the training of their students, emphasizing the linguistic abilities that may not be the strength of students who are well on their way to becoming extremely qualified as skilled plumbers or electricians. In the summer of 2001, a Massachusetts legislator proposed a bill "calling for vocational students to be exempted from passing the MCAS in order to get a high school diploma" (Alice Giordano, *Boston Globe*, July 1, 2001, p. 1). In a further development, according to an August 30 article in the Boston Herald.com (www.bostonherald.com) by Ellen J. Silberman, high school seniors who have availed themselves of extra help from the school system but who have nevertheless failed the MCAS repeatedly would be eligible for "$1000 in state grants to get tutoring" (p. 1) outside the school bureaucracy. In Florida, a group called FCAR (Florida Coalition for Assessment Reform) has formed to protest against the state's Florida Comprehensive Assessment Test (FCAT).

A member of FCAR, Gloria Pipkin, is quoted saying, "FCAT cannibalizes the curriculum, diverts scarce resources, discriminates against those who don't test well, and turns schools into giant test prep centers" (Alisa Ulferts, *St. Petersburg Times*, July 3, 2001, p. 1).

Kathy Slobogin in a CNN.com/Education article on July 23, 2001, wrote that an unintended and "unwelcome side effect—cheating" is emerging as a result of high-stakes testing. She cites schools in Michigan, Maryland, New York City, and Austin, Texas, as examples of this. This is not a case of one teacher or principal here and there. In Michigan, seventy-one schools in twenty-two districts were cited. In Austin, the "tampering with test scores" was spread across the city, and the case went to criminal court (pp. 1–2). When promotion, prestige, salary, and even one's job depend on a single test, the temptation is to do whatever it takes to get good test results. Each year following the latest round of tests, allegations, and rumors of cheating abound. Gerald Bracey in *Bail Me Out!—Handling Difficult Data and Tough Questions about Public Schools*, states that in 1998 "the superintendent of Alexandria, Virginia, public schools received a contract with a clause calling for bonuses if test scores rose by a certain amount" (Corwin Press, Inc., 2000, p. 100). I have no idea what happened in Alexandria, but I suppose the pressure on principals and teachers to have students perform well on tests may have been ferocious.

The most recent Federal Education Law calls for reading and mathematics to be tested each year in grades 3 to 8. Of course, each of the fifty states will use a different test and somewhat different standards. Some tests will be rigorous and others less so. Some states will require a passing score of 50, but others will require 55 or 60 or 65, or even 70. The test results, therefore, will tell us very little about whether a student in New York is at the same standard as a student in Texas or Oregon, although there will be some connection to the NAEP that may make crude comparisons possible. In the end, the tests may tell us a great deal about the politics in individual states and the degree to which various pressure groups in those states got what they wanted.

Many state commissioners, superintendents of schools and governors are very worried about the new tests on the grounds that they will not provide any diagnostic information that will help an individual student, they will be expensive to administer and score—perhaps taking money away from other areas of the education budget—they will not be fair to all areas of a complex state, and they will once again reveal that certain schools and students need far more help than others, but no funds or inadequate funds will be available to provide that help. Of course, there is also a political dimension to all of this: rigorous tests will reveal problems and embarrass elected officials; easy tests will make the politicians look good but paper over the problems of inadequate education that eventually get revealed when we learn that high school students cannot do sixth-grade math or reading.

One of the most difficult problems is getting accurate measures when not all students are tested. States have their own policies for exemption: certain special education students, students who are not native speakers of English, students who have not been in the particular school or district more than three or six or nine months, and on and on. Test scores may influence anything from school reputations to local real estate values, so districts have a strong incentive to report good scores. One way to do that is to hold back poor students the year before a major test. This goes on in many states from Texas to Massachusetts, in ninth grade, for instance, the year before a major test in tenth grade. Professor Walt Haney, an education professor at Boston College, said, "When schools are held accountable in terms of examinations pass rates, they will fail kids in the grade before the examination" (John Mcelhenny, Associated Press, November 14, 2001, Boston.com.home, p. 1).

Required state tests are successful when they are aligned with important standards and curriculum that provides material to get at those standards. Recently, two prestigious board members of Achieve, Inc., a nonprofit consulting firm, asked Achieve to evaluate some of the states' tests to see how close the alignment was between standards and what was actually tested. The board members were Governor John Engler of Michigan and IBM Chairman Louis V. Gerstner Jr., and the results were not heartening. According to Richard Rothstein (*New York Times*, May 1, 2002, A21), "Achieve found that most tests are poorly matched to state standards."

The states are doing a good job testing the smaller skills, but often do not test more sophisticated material in their own standards. As an example, Rothstein cites a Minnesota fifth-grade reading standard that expects pupils to identify both the main idea and supporting details in a passage. "But the states' test emphasizes identification of details, not the main idea." Rothstein concludes that as teachers learn that this is the game, they will train students to concentrate on small details and "will not do much to train students in higher-order thinking" such as how to discern the main idea in a paragraph.

There are solutions to these and other problems. First, education must become a very high budget priority. That will allow schools to improve the lot of youngsters in disadvantaged schools and to include many more testing opportunities where students can write essays, present work they have done in math or English, and display or perform work where that is appropriate. All of these things can be assessed quite accurately—in fact, they are assessed every day in the marketplace. Second, the standards must focus on the most important things we want our youngsters to learn, the curriculum must accurately reflect those standards, and the assessment must reflect what the standards and curriculum contain. That could mean that in secondary schools the tests are not the same for all students—the point that the advocates of a very different set of tests for vocational students are making in Massachusetts.

Writing would be a good example. If we say we want our children to be able to write well in many forms from reactions to pictures in the early grades to laboratory reports, short narratives, and position papers as they get older, we must establish that as a standard, give our children many opportunities to learn about and write those different kinds of papers, and allow them to write several times for diagnostic assessment so we can see how well they are doing and figure out ways to help them. In some schools, that might mean somewhat smaller classes so teachers can carefully and thoughtfully read the writing through its stages. Almost no one in the real world writes anything serious on demand. Writing goes through revisions, and even skilled professional writers have editors. Only on school tests do we sample knowledge of technical aspects of writing or look at a single short piece of work done under extreme pressure and say that is a fair indicator of writing ability. Worse, of course, are indirect tests where we ask students questions about the rules of writing and grammar, but we don't actually look at their writing. Imagine a symphony orchestra giving a position to the person who could correctly answer the most questions about a violin or a flute, but never asked him or her to play the instrument.

WHAT DO I NEED TO KNOW ABOUT CLASS SIZE?

DISCUSSION

There is a commonly held belief among many teachers that smaller class size results in more and better learning for students, and this may be true. There have been hundreds of studies on the subject over the years and no clear agreement because it matters how a class is run. A very simple example would be that seminars and cooperative learning groups need different sizes from lectures. While this is a complicated issue, there are a couple of things that can be said with reasonable certainty.

PERSPECTIVE AND DETAILS

First, if you measure learning almost exclusively with multiple choice or short answer tests, there may be little difference in classes with fifteen students and those with twenty, twenty-five, or even thirty students. If the tests are high-stakes, the teachers will spend considerable time familiarizing students with the test format and drilling them in what they must know on the day of the test. There will be reduced effort to have students solve original problems, learn to work in groups,

write paragraphs or essays about their work, or do any other higher order tasks that would lead to sophisticated learning. This is not because
teachers do not want to do these things, but the pressure is on for many
months of the school year to prepare children for high-stakes tests.

Pundits often say teachers should still do sophisticated lessons and
the tests do not restrict teachers as much as they claim. However, the
fact remains that either the pundits are wrong, or teachers and school-
level administrators are sufficiently frightened by high-stakes tests that
the majority of administrators and teachers tell researchers conducting
confidential surveys that they feel they must drill and drill to get students ready for the big day.

Second, within reason, it is not the number of students in a class, but
the "behavior" of the students in the class that counts. In a *New York
Times* article (February 22, 2001) summarizing research by Professor
Edward Lazear of Stanford University, Virginia Postrel reported that
"the key variable is how likely it is that students disrupt one another's
learning. (This disruption can occur through classic misbehavior; it can
take the form of asking questions the students already know the answers
to.) Small differences in behavior can have large effects on learning and
big implications for class size" (p. 2).

The point here is that it is the level of "disruption" that counts and
that the disruptions need not be behavioral problems, but can just as
easily be frequent questions from an insecure student or volunteered information from a very bright youngster who offers information whether
the teacher asks for it or not. Any principal can tell you that most teachers would prefer a first-grade class of twenty-two well-behaved, reasonably bright and reasonably compliant youngsters to a class of twelve serious behavior problems without regard to intelligence. Teachers with
seniority in high school often opt for larger classes, particularly honors
and AP classes, over much smaller classes with "remedial skills" or "difficult" students.

There are actions that can be taken to make class size an effective tool
in school improvement, but they require a mature understanding of the
problem and the will to at least consider a number of things.

First, it is generally better to have smaller than larger classes. There
will usually be fewer chances for disruption, the teacher will feel better
about the class, and students will have more opportunities to gain the

teacher's attention. In Tennessee's Project STAR, for instance, a serious research effort to measure the effect of class size, Dr. David C. Illig reported in a paper dated June 11, 1996 (available from the California Research Bureau, Sacramento, CA 95841) that "children in smaller classes consistently out-performed children in larger classes. The average achievement differential was about twice the amount expected based on estimates published in the literature" (p. 3). This study took into account inner-city, small city, suburban, and rural children who were randomly placed, as were their teachers, in classes of thirteen to seventeen, or classes of twenty-two to twenty-five elementary students. For readers interested in much more information about Project STAR and arguments in favor of reducing class size, take a look at Charles M. Achilles' *Let's Put Kids First, Finally: Getting Class Size Right* (Corwin Press, Inc, 1999).

Where large classes are unavoidable, attention should be paid to the students who are likely to be disruptive, and class size should be modified to counter that problem. It makes no sense for all classes to be the same size. Classes that present more problems for the teacher should be smaller than those classes that have more "typical" students.

Again, disruptive does not necessarily mean ill-behaved; "problems" and "typical" are not code words for majority or minority. Disruptive means that a child will make special demands on the teacher because the student is unusually creative, has problems with impulse control, needs to ask many questions, is behind in reading, has a learning disability, or any of a host of other reasons. That child might count as 1.5 children in a classroom. Children who have a history of working well in a class or in groups should be considered typical and could count as 1.0. In an elementary school, some "heterogeneous" classes could be as small as fourteen or sixteen and others as large as twenty-two or twenty-four. Again, to be careful here, this is not an argument for any form of segregation or homogeneous grouping. It is an argument for adjusting class size to recognize that some students are more disruptive than others and that those disruptive students may be among the brightest and most creative youngsters in a class.

Class size matters most in settings that favor "powerful learning": cooperative learning, performance tasks, problem-based learning, thoughtful and variable assessment, as four examples. Adherents of powerful learning techniques[1] strongly believe that the opportunity for sophisticated and deep learning increases when learning is decentralized in a controlled and planned manner, but this often depends on having classes of modest size. Of course, class size also matters in traditional classrooms, but the chance for disruption increases when classes are decentralized. Students have more opportunities to interact with each other and the teacher as well as increased opportunities to take some initiative. Disruptive students need to learn how to operate in groups or pairs, and this will take time and smaller classes.

NOTE

1. Ronald S. Brandt, *Powerful Learning*, ASCD, 1998

II

ALTERNATIVES TO TRADITIONAL PUBLIC AND PRIVATE EDUCATION: VOUCHERS, CHARTER SCHOOLS, AND HOME SCHOOLING

This part examines the following questions.

Question 5: What do I need to know about vouchers?
Question 6: What do I need to know about charter schools?
Question 7: What do I need to know about home schooling?

As recently as twenty years ago, virtually every American student was enrolled in a public or private school for all of his or her K–12 instruction. To be sure, the public schools varied in everything from size to culture; the private schools might be secular or religious, and they also had substantial variety. But considerably more than 99 percent of our students were in public schools, for the most part in their neighborhood, or private schools chosen by parents who could afford that particular school or did what they must to enroll their child in a private school that favored a method of instruction or religion those parents felt was of great importance to their family.

That is now changing. For several years, there has been a national debate about choice in schools—perhaps even giving every parent the full range of choice. Vouchers and charter schools have become part of the educational landscape, and the home schooling movement has grown a great deal. While the vast majority of students—perhaps 97 percent— are still in those same public and private schools, the number of families exercising choice and considering choice is increasing far more rapidly than general school enrollment. The number of students using a voucher, attending a charter school, or receiving home instruction is close to two million in 2002.

Many people favor vouchers as a way to give parents considerable leverage over the way instruction is offered in the schools. Voucher adherents believe that if parents are granted enough tuition money, they will either cause the public schools of their choice to operate precisely as they wish—and that will certainly vary from community to community and even from house to house in many neighborhoods—or they will be able to send their child to a private school that operates as they wish. Charter school adherents believe they should be able to petition the state to form a new school around their proposed criteria within the public system, but without some of the restrictions and regulations of the public school. Parents who prefer home schooling go even further in their desire to educate their child as they please. Believing that the family is the central educational unit and that they should be able to teach a child exactly what that family wishes, they simply keep their child at home and, with appropriate help, educate the child there.

This part will provide you with a basic understanding of these important issues and some sense of the direction they are taking.

5

WHAT DO I NEED TO KNOW ABOUT VOUCHERS?

DISCUSSION

Vouchers may eventually be an integral part of the education landscape, but they are clearly not the answer to all of education's ills, real or imagined. However, the voucher concept is an interesting and controversial addition to the education conversation. Basically, parents receive a voucher or credit for a specified number of dollars they could use to educate their K–12 children. Some people think vouchers should be used to help parents pay tuition in private or religious schools; others think vouchers should be issued for the full amount of tuition at such schools. Still other people think vouchers should be issued to allow new schools to be developed or to enable students to pay tuition in nearby public schools at the going per-pupil rate.

PERSPECTIVE AND DETAILS

There are approximately fifty-three million K–12 children in the United States. Some children are home schooled, others are in tuition schools (secular private or religious private), but the vast majority (over 95 percent) of children are in public schools. Many public schools are doing very well; some public schools are not doing well. Many parents agree with the culture in their public schools; some parents do not agree with the prevailing culture in their child's school. It is chiefly poor parents whose children are not in good schools or parents who very much want some particular theme or culture in their child's school who have the greatest interest in vouchers.

Many schools in the inner-cities of this country have been struggling or failing for years, even decades. How long must these students and parents wait for their schools to improve? Wouldn't it be fair to give these parents full-tuition vouchers, or at least substantial tuition vouchers, if the school has had a failing record for three or more consecutive years by some established local or state standard? This would allow those parents to choose a private or religious school or even a nearby public school in an adjoining district that was willing to take a tuition student. Of course, there is considerable debate about what, exactly, constitutes "failing" and just how long a school must be in the failing category to make its students eligible for vouchers.

How much money should parents be granted for a voucher—enough to enroll their child in a religious school, a nearby public school, an elite private school? Should vouchers be partial or full? Should the parents pay 10 percent, 40 percent, or more of the tuition? What about providing transportation or reimbursing families for other school expenses such as books, supplies, and field trips? John Goodlad has another take on vouchers that would enhance a youngster's education in his or her current school. "He would allow youngsters, particularly those in small schools, to use up to 10% of the cost of their education in that district for special training that is not available in the school" (Mark F. Goldberg, "Leadership for Change: An Interview with John Goodlad," Phi Delta Kappan, September 2000, p. 85). This might provide eligible students with vouchers for anything from math tutoring to violin lessons.

Are there enough seats in local schools, public or private, for the students to find acceptance? Do we have any evidence that these schools will be willing to accept students from failing schools or from good schools where their parents simply do not agree with the school's culture? Does anyone believe, for instance, that the many high-tuition private schools in our nation's cities, populated largely by children from affluent families, will suddenly open their doors to dozens or hundreds of poor children from underperforming schools just because they have vouchers?

Right now, we have a multi-billion dollar problem with schools all over the country that are somewhat outmoded and particularly ill-quipped for twenty-first century wiring—or even dangerously decrepit. How can we build new schools or renovate old ones quickly enough that might be able to handle many new students if we start issuing vouchers? It makes little sense to send dozens of ill-prepared students or students whose parents are unhappy with the schools their children attend now to a school physically not set up to handle this influx.

What will be the effect of vouchers on the public school system? It is clear that vouchers cannot cover the tuition of more than a small number of students, at least for the foreseeable future. Will we create a new set of schools that duplicate all or many of the problems of the schools that were unsatisfactory? There is no way in a year or a decade—or even in twenty-five or thirty years—to dismantle the huge public school system or go to a complete choice system. Of course, reasonable people might question how many people would actually opt for a different school, since the vast majority of the parents of school-age children when asked in the annual Gallup Poll conducted for Phi Delta Kappa express confidence in the schools their children now attend. It's usually the "other schools" that have the problems.

In the next several years, we'll have a better picture of how vouchers work or could work. There are already voucher programs or proposals for such programs everywhere from Milwaukee to Cleveland, from Maine to Vermont. Professor Henry Levin at Teachers College, Columbia University, is the Director of the National Center for the Study of Privatization in Education, the honest broker in the effort to determine the effects of all forms of school privatization. Of course, other organizations from the Rand Corporation to the Center on Education Policy, both based in the nation's capital, are interested in this topic, have reported on it, but have yet to locate any research that is strong enough to base a conclusion on. Privatization can include for-profit schools, vouchers, and other methods that, for the most part, focus on the problem of how to help families in neighborhoods with poorly performing schools. Right now, the central issue in the privatization effort is vouchers. This center will accumulate data and report from time-to-time on issues related to privatization in an effort to see if student performance improves and to determine how various programs work.

Vouchers are still in a very early stage, many new programs will be tried in the coming years, and considerable research will surely be done by both partisans and more objective researchers. It is fair to say, however, that to date "The research on vouchers . . . has failed to show any but the most modest and equivocal gains for participating students" (Kenneth Howe, Margaret Eisenhart, and Damian Betebenner, "School Choice Crucible: A Case Study of Boulder Valley," Phi Delta *Kappan*, October 2001, p. 146). This particular statement by these three authors was based on the examination of three recent articles in respectable journals.

Will vouchers hurt, or even destroy, the public school system? If you have five hundred youngsters in an elementary school and through a voucher program across grades, fifty of those youngsters' families elect to use vouchers for tuition schools, under many programs the public school loses 10 percent of its financing, but has no way to cut its insurance or heat or light bill by 10 percent and probably can't even reduce its payroll very much unless most of the students are taken out of one or two grades. How can this be managed in a way that helps both the public school and the parents who are dissatisfied? What will happen to the students who remain in the public school system, but have fewer dollars to support their education?

Will parents at some future time be eligible for "virtual vouchers?" If, for instance, parents could gain a tax deduction of, say, up to $10,000 per year for K–12 nonpublic school expenses or get a tax credit for several thousand dollars, that would give parents, and particularly middle and upper-middle class parents, a virtual voucher.

Vouchers were not included in the latest Education Bill passed by the Congress in 2001, but they are certain to remain an issue in many cities and states and could be included, in some form, in future education legislation at the federal level.

6

WHAT DO I NEED TO
KNOW ABOUT CHARTER SCHOOLS?

DISCUSSION

The charter school movement is growing rapidly, so it is not possible to say with any certainty how many states are involved and how many schools are charter schools. By the 2000–2001 school year, at least thirty-five states had at least one charter school and at least twelve hundred charter schools were in operation, many of them quite small—one hundred to two hundred students. There are new groups forming every school year to propose charter schools, although this is still a modest movement with, perhaps, two hundred thousand students involved. The national interest is strong enough to say that while this or that charter school may not survive, the concept is here to stay.

Charter schools are an effort by some group of parents, community members, educators, or other interested parties to form a school that offers an alternative to the existing public schools in their area, yet the charter school remains within the public school system in that it is subject to state and federal laws, it uses public school funds, it is open to all students, and it may not discriminate in any way that violates state and federal laws. However, charter schools are free to petition for relief from some state or contractual obligations. Charter schools may serve students in any grades from K–12.

The new charter school could emphasize experiential education, highly traditional basic education, or environmental education; it could be organized around a math-science emphasis, a business preparation curriculum, or a vocational program; it could be built on the tenets of the Core Knowledge Curriculum or Howard Gardner's multiple intelligences concept or the values and guidelines of the Coalition of Essential Schools. There really are no limits to the possible themes of charter schools. The school may serve students in grades K–3 or 6–8 or any other combination of grades.

PERSPECTIVE AND DETAILS

Charter schools operate on the theory that the best schools are directly responsive to the needs of the children in those schools. When the school must answer to school boards, teacher unions, or state agencies, the needs of the children may not be served as well as they should be. Charter schools are formed by people who wish to serve the needs of children and their parents who want a particular kind of school and are willing to take serious steps to get that school. The interested parties meet, draw up a mission statement, go through a demanding list of state requirements, submit their proposal to the state's approving authority, and begin a new school if the proposal is approved.

Again, the charter schools vary greatly in their theme and appeal. In Dunedin, Florida, the charter school includes weekly classes in dance, drama, music, and visual art. In St. Paul, Minnesota, one charter school emphasizes a nonviolent way of life in a racially and culturally diverse school. Other schools work with disruptive students, students who want a content-rich curriculum taught in a traditional manner or students who are pregnant or are teenage mothers.

Charter schools have to consider all students who apply for admission. Typically, charter schools submit a plan in their proposal for how students will be admitted. Many charter schools use a lottery if more students apply than can be accommodated. Of course, because the schools have a strong theme, they usually attract parents and students who strongly want that particular approach to schooling. There is the danger that these schools could intensify stratification by extremely narrowly defined objectives that attract students of one race or one very specific religious practice, something that broad-based public schools usually avoid.

Charter schools may apply for waivers from a host of the usual regulations. They can be free of many teacher union or state test constraints, may require a longer school day, and may even require a certain level of parent involvement in the school. They cannot charge tuition and, again, may not discriminate on the basis of ethnicity, national origin, gender, or disability; these are still public schools.

Some charter schools are successful by most measures, some charter schools are successful by their own measures, and other charter schools have failed and have not had their charters renewed by the state. The movement is about ten years old, and many schools have been in operation five or fewer years, so it is too early to tell how well they do what they say they will do. Because the schools vary so much, they must be judged individually. Charter schools may get hurt by the enthusiasm for using prescribed standardized tests as the measure of a school's performance. Charter schools, by their nature, focus on their special mission, yet they will often be measured by how well students do on tests of standard content, pitting their special curriculum against the state-mandated content—even though they have a charter. Of course, they could apply for a waiver, but then the dilemma is that there is no way to compare them to other schools.

Many groups, including teacher organizations, are not enthusiastic about charter schools on the grounds that the charter teachers are not always well trained and state certified, that they do not play on a level field because they are excused from many requirements the other public schools must submit to, and that they are often training young people in a very narrow way—around a theme that means much to a small group but may not serve students in the broader world. Some people may even object strenuously to the theme of a particular charter school and feel it does not belong inside the public system.

Another criticism of charter schools is that they detract from the need to make all public schools excellent. Once parents are involved in a charter school, they tend to give their passion to that school and have less interest in the whole local system.

In a 1999 article titled "Not All Charter Schools Are Created Equal," in *Focus on the Family* magazine, Dick M. Carpenter II made the following recommendations to parents looking into a charter school:

1. Ask questions about the method of instruction, the curriculum, the classroom culture, homework policy, and the testing and grading procedures.
2. Learn about such support services as counseling, family involvement, and the breakfast and lunch programs or facilities.
3. Find out about co-curricular activities, the arts and physical education, and any special federal programs.
4. Find out how the school is governed. How is the school supervised? Is the governing board responsive to the parents' and the community's needs?
5. Get all the information you can from the school's mission statement, newsletters, brochures, policy statements, and other material that is available.

Adherents of the charter school movement are typically interested in standards, accountability, and assessments that suit the needs of their particular school. Parents and others devoted to choice within the public schools or devoted to a particular charter school are passionate about what they are doing, particularly since this choice movement, unlike vouchers, is inside the public system. Charter schools, whatever your opinion, are now part of the public school landscape and show every sign of remaining there. It is simply a matter of determining which of these schools thrive and which do not. Because charter schools rely on continued parental interest and support—unlike regular public schools, which serve all students within a cachement area—they can grow, falter or simply go out of business.

7

WHAT DO I NEED TO
KNOW ABOUT HOME SCHOOLING?

DISCUSSION

Home schooling is an especially controversial subject, one that quickly becomes highly emotional for many people. When advocates write about home schooling they sometimes refer to "government schools" rather than public schools or they talk about "learning in freedom" and the equation between compulsory school attendance and militaristic government. Opponents of home schooling are equally hard-line, if somewhat less dramatic. The National Education Association (NEA) states in a formal resolution "that home schooling programs cannot provide the student with a comprehensive education experience." The resolution goes on to say that "home-schooled students should not participate in any extra-curricular activities in the public schools" and that the public schools should determine grade placement and credits for work done at home (National Education Association, NEA 2000–2001 Resolutions, B-68. Home Schooling).

Home schooling is a very real and serious part of the educational landscape today, something that could not have been said as recently as twenty years ago when the number of students educated at home was something like one-fifth of 1 percent of the school-age population. The

National Center for Education Statistics (NCES) of the U.S. Department of Education in its abstract of the report titled "Home Schooling in the United States: 1999" states that in the spring of 1999, "an estimated 850,000 students nationwide were being homeschooled" (NCES, Product Information Page, nces.ed.gov). Since home schooling, in the view of both advocates and opponents, is now growing at a rate of 5 to 15 percent each year, it is safe to say that in 2002 more than one million youngsters received all or most of their school instruction at home—about 2 percent of all K–12 students. Home schooling is legal in all fifty states, and it is an acceptable method of education that can lead to accomplishment—including winning national contests or gaining admission to good and excellent colleges. If anyone doubts the growing importance of home schooling, that doubter has only to look at the August 27, 2001 issue of *Time* magazine where "Is Home Schooling Good for America?" was the cover story.

PERSPECTIVE AND DETAILS

The first thing to know about home schooling is that the reasons for keeping youngsters at home and both the quality and nature of at-home instruction vary a great deal. There may be a combination of factors in the decision to keep children at home, but most families list one of the following as the deciding factor: quality of education issues, religious issues, socialization issues, and parenting and family issues.

Quality of Education Issues

A major complaint of parents who opt to home school their children is that the public schools are lacking in academic rigor. These parents claim they can do a better job at home. This is very difficult to assess since there are no national norms for evaluating these students. Home schoolers constantly cite the occasional winners of national spelling bee contests or science competitions as well as acceptance of a few outstanding home-schooled students at Harvard or Stanford or MIT. Supervision of home-schooled students varies enormously: in New York, these students are under the careful scrutiny of local public school districts, but in Texas they are hardly regulated or supervised at all. Almost all of the available evidence suggests that the parents of home-schooled students are "better educated than the adult population at large, and the family will be comfortably middle class" (Brian Anderson, "City Journal," Summer 2000, v. 10, no. 3, p. 2); therefore, one would suspect that the youngsters would do well in any serious educational setting, and home-schooling parents are typically highly motivated to do a good job.

These are often angry parents who agree with William J. Bennett, Chester E. Finn Jr., and John T. E. Cribb Jr. who argue in their book *The Educated Child: A Parent's Guide* (Simon & Schuster, 1999) that public schools have let parents down in the last thirty years by not insisting on high standards, highly trained and motivated teachers, and a high moral tone. Of course, public school advocates insist that many schools are better than ever as a result of reforms that include critical thinking, new state standards and assessments, cooperative learning, and an appreciation of the growing diversity in the American population.

Home-schooled students are not left to their own and their parents' devices. There are many secular and religious organizations that supply books, materials, CD-ROMs, online services, kits, and daily or weekly curriculum guides that emphasize their organization's particular educational philosophy. William Bennett, the former U.S. Secretary of Education and public education critic, is marketing an online, for-profit, home schooling program called K12. For all students, but particularly secondary-age students, parents sometimes pool their knowledge, engage tutors, or enroll their youngsters in a community college or even a public or private school course. Obviously, it is easier to conduct instruction in the lower grades. When young people need upper-level instruction in math, language, art, computer technology, or science, for instance, parents use other available resources.

Strong public school advocates argue that home-schooled children do not have access to certified teachers who are experts in the teaching of reading, mathematics, physics, or advanced drawing. Neither do these students have easy access to the range of opportunities and equipment a public school can provide—from various sports to computers, from

musical instruments to interaction with youngsters with a variety of attitudes and backgrounds. Of course, public school advocates also object
to the loss of funds for students not in public schools and the loss of support for public school from families who have no stake in the schools.
One compromise, emerging more and more, is for home-schooled children to take one course or participate in one co-curricular activity in a
local public school.

Religious Issues

Many parents of home-schooled children object to the separation of
church and state. They want their children to learn a great deal about
their religion, the role of religion in U.S. history in general, and they
want a strong moral point of view—meaning the point of view they es-
pouse. They object to schools that do not permit prayer or are tolerant
of, say, gay and lesbian parents. According to Brian C. Anderson, the
typical home-schooling family "is likely to be white (only 6 percent of
home-schooling families are minorities) and observantly Christian, with
married parents and three or more kids . . ." ("City Journal," Summer
2000, v. 10. no. 3, p. 2).

These individuals want their youngsters exposed predominantly to a
particular point of view they favor. That is not possible in a public
school, and they probably don't have a private school they like in their
area or can't afford the tuition. While youngsters of every religion and
no religion are home schooled, the largest home-schooled group remains Christian, and they find much that is objectionable in the public
schools. They strongly object to what they perceive as the tolerant (They
might say "lax" or "irresponsible") attitude of public school administrators and teachers who accept variations on family life or beliefs about
moral issues that are anathema to these people with strong convictions
about what is right and wrong. These are very serious people willing to
make " a galactic commitment of time and money and patience" (John
Cloud and Jodie Morse, *Time*, August 27, 2001, p. 49) to keep their children at home. This commitment, of course, is also one of the limiting
factors in the home-schooling movement. There is probably a natural
cap on this movement's growth related to the time and resources necessary for parents to educate children at home.

Socialization Issues

Most advocates of home schooling and public education agree on this issue, although they often differ in the details. Youngsters do need to interact with other young people and do need to learn how to operate in the real world where people have differences. Public school advocates argue that theirs is the best and most natural setting in which that can occur. Students must get along with all of the students in their classes and co-curricular activities or on their athletic teams—not to mention students they may have contact with in nearby communities through various school activities. Because of the nature of the public schools, there are no restrictions on the backgrounds of the youngsters. A child may be in a class with a child of any religion, belief, or nationality, a child who is homeless or the child of the most affluent family in town. Home-schooling advocates argue that their youngsters are scouts, members of 4-H clubs, local orchestras, religious groups, and charitable volunteer groups. They, of course, can choose the activities, groups, and settings from which they feel their children can benefit or are ready for at a particular time.

Parenting and Family Issues

Chris Jeub, a certified English teacher in Minnesota who has chosen home schooling for his own children, wrote in *Educational Leadership* in September 1994 that "Home-school parents see the family as superior to any other institution in society. When the education institution threatens the family, these parents tend to choose to educate their children at home" (p. 51). Jeub does not take an alarmist position on this or any other topic and concedes that there are many good things about public education, but makes the case that many "home-school parents choose to take their children out of school because of the school's teachings on sensitive issues like premarital sex, same-sex relationships, questioning of authority, and secular religion" (p. 51).

Advocates of home schooling see the movement as protecting youngsters from a popular culture that inundates them with images of violence, promiscuity, and defiance of proper authority. They worry about what they see as the general decline in adult leadership, relativistic presentation of moral values, and a general lack of strong discipline in the schools. Advocates of public education often argue that it is not protection that the youngsters get, but insulation from a very complex and real world—the one in which these students must ultimately live. They also argue that school personnel are overwhelmingly decent citizens who enforce proper discipline.

Much like vouchers and charter schools, home schooling is now a significant and growing part of the educational repertoire. Given the number of students involved, over the next several years, without question, there will some independent research studies to determine how these students do on everything from standardized tests and college acceptances compared to students of similar ability and from similar socio-economic backgrounds. Stay tuned for new information.

III

TEACHING AND LEARNING:
EIGHT INNOVATIONS

This section examines the following questions.

Question 8: What are differentiated instruction, problem-based learning, and multiple intelligences?

Question 9: What are constructivism and content-rich curriculum?

Question 10: What are teacher portfolios?

Question 11: What is the best way to educate Limited English Proficient (LEP) students?

Question 12: What do I need to know about rubrics?

Without question, another writer might have eliminated one or two of these questions and substituted others. My four criteria for what to include were fairly simple:

- The method or technique has been used with some degree of success in at least hundreds of school districts, and perhaps many more, in the past twenty years.

  Rubrics and LEP issues are good examples of the national interest. Many states now use *rubrics* for assessment, and workshops are held all over the country on rubrics in an effort to familiarize practitioners with what they are and how they work—and sometimes with how they are constructed. California and Arizona, by law, have instituted new methods for helping LEP students, and there is growing interest in this new method, Structured English Immersion (SEI), in dozens of places from New York City to Colorado.

- Books and articles have recently been written about each of these subjects. You will learn from reading this section the authors and titles of several of these works. When different publishers and editors begin sponsoring or soliciting articles and books on a subject, that is a sure indicator of widespread and developing interest in those subjects.

- These topics are on the agenda of many educational organizations at their local and national conferences. Most of these questions appear in some form in the conference bulletins of such large gatherings of educators as American Education Research Association (AERA) and Association for Supervision and Curriculum Development (ASCD). Often, smaller organizations will focus on a single topic at a meeting. The Core Knowledge Foundation, for instance, focuses almost exclusively on content-rich curriculum.

- These are general methods, topics, or questions that cut across subject areas and grades as opposed to very specific questions about the teaching of science or music or language arts.

In the end, of course, I made the final selections for what to include as questions. Based on traveling, researching my own books, editing books, reading education books, reading the journals and magazines in the field, attending conferences, and talking to teachers, administrators, publishers, parents and others, I concluded that the issues captured in these questions are important, complex, and too often misunderstood or incompletely understood.

WHAT ARE
DIFFERENTIATED INSTRUCTION,
PROBLEM-BASED LEARNING,
AND MULTIPLE INTELLIGENCES?

DISCUSSION

Differentiated instruction (DI), problem-based learning (PBL), and multiple intelligences (MI) are three important methods of recognizing that students differ in readiness to learn, vary in their best ways to master new knowledge, bring different life experiences to the classroom, often profit from grappling with questions that have no one clear answer, and frequently display mastery using multiple forms of expression. Asking students to learn the same things at the same pace in the same way flies in the face of everything we have learned in the past seventy-five years about child development and learning.

PERSPECTIVE AND DETAILS

While there are many legitimate curriculums, approaches, standards, and tests that require students to master a certain body of knowledge, it is very unlikely that schools can cause large groups of students, especially diverse students, to master that knowledge in a lock-step manner or in a short space of time: six months or one year. The state of Michigan, for instance, announced in early 2001 that 20 percent of their schools may not be meeting new state standards. Our knowledge of child development tells us that while there can be low-stakes local tests of various kinds as often as teachers and others feel they are needed, high-stakes tests should be given at intervals of about three years. Some children enter kindergarten able to read; most children learn to read in the first grade; almost all children can be taught to read reasonably well by the end of the second grade; a very few children won't read until the third grade. An arbitrary high-stakes test in reading in the sixth-month of the first grade will likely reveal at least as much about development as about ability to read.

Learning styles and learning paces vary in even relatively homogeneous school populations. In a book published in early 2002, Gayle H. Gregory and Carolyn Chapman state that often "teachers have spent summers writing and designing curriculum that focuses on standards and is intended to engage learners. But when they met the students in the classroom, the program didn't fit their needs or appeal to them" (*Differential Instructional Strategies: One Size Doesn't Fit All*, Corwin Press, Inc., p. 19). As the authors go on to say, it's as if someone sent the wrong students.

In spite of the desires of many politicians and other lay people, educators know that no single curriculum or set of learning exercises will work with a school population as diverse as ours. Again, teachers, schools, and districts can administer tests for strictly diagnostic purposes in the interim, but tests that determine who gets promoted or which teachers, principals, or schools are rewarded should not be given at one-year or shorter intervals. Differentiated instruction, problem-based learning, and multiple intelligences can help in the effort to vary the method and pace of instruction, yet respect important standards that have been developed around the country.

Differentiated Instruction

This philosophy of instruction recognizes that students arrive in the classroom with different levels of everything from information and deep knowledge to readiness to learn, life experiences, and specific talents for learning and expressing that learning. Carol Ann Tomlinson says in her

1999 ASCD book *The Differentiated Classroom: Responding to the Needs of All Learners* that "teachers begin where students are, not the front of a curriculum guide" (p. 2). Millions of students move from one location to another each year, sometimes across state lines, in a nation where there is no national curriculum, and where frequently there is substantial variation in the curriculum from district to district within a state. Individual states, largely for local political reasons, guard their control of education quite fiercely. Because of the very real differences among communities and states, there likely will not and should not be a national curriculum in the foreseeable future, so students arrive at their new school ahead or behind in several curriculum areas. Students constantly enter our schools from other countries, and sometimes do not speak English at all or with any degree of fluency. These facts on top of developmental and other inherent differences render a set curriculum within a short period of time folly for a majority of our students.

Teams of teachers and whole schools need to devote staff development time to creating a variety of approaches and lessons to accommodate these many differences. No elementary teacher, for example, on his or her own can create enough opportunities for youngsters of different abilities and linguistic backgrounds. It is important to create the mindset that individual needs must be accommodated as much as humanly possible and that it will take the whole staff to create and constantly renew a complex and changing curriculum and the effective teaching materials to support that curriculum.

In many classrooms—and surely in cities and large, close-in suburbs—student background and readiness to learn vary enormously. Some students come from homes in which excellent education is a family tradition; other students have parents who have had very little education. Some students were born in the community where they are now in second or fourth grades; others arrived a year ago from a distant state or another country. Of course, there are also differences in abilities, skills, attitudes, and aptitudes. You probably cannot teach the same math or language arts material to all of these students in the same way and at the same pace. Differentiated instruction adherents promote flexible approaches to accommodate academic diversity. By using learning centers, graphic organizers, pantomime, learning groups, performances and exhibitions, independent study, computer programs, multiple texts, and other techniques,

DI teachers can develop student talent to the point where either some whole-group methods can be used or students and teachers will simply discover what works best for an individual or a small group of students.

If we do not accommodate diverse learners, we will continue the trend of the latest (year 2000) National Assessment of Educational Progress (NAEP) results. According to Michael Kelly in the April 11, 2001, *Washington Post*, "The NAEP confirmed that we are continuing to create a nation radically divided along meritocratic lines. The top level is held by a tiny, hyper-schooled and highly competent overclass" (A27). These are the most advantaged students who can master a set curriculum. Many other students perform reasonably well on the NAEP tests, but literally millions of our students in grades K–12 are not able to master the skills tested on the NAEP well enough to succeed in school, to get decent jobs, or to contribute in any serious way to their own well-being or the economic growth of our country. Kelly goes on to say, "A stunning 60 percent of poor children and minority children are shoveled through the schools and out the other end, largely illiterate and innumerate" (A27). We keep inventing new standards and tests when we need to craft dozens of ways to help these young people master the standards and skills that will help them lead satisfying lives and contribute to the larger society.

Problem-Based Learning (PBL)

This instructional method presents students with a problem or challenge that does not have an obvious or single answer. Young children might be presented with the problem of designing an exhibit on a local Indian tribe for display in a nearby town hall. They research the tribe (history and sociology), learn about physical exhibit space limits and appropriate math (math and some science), design an effective and esthetically pleasing layout (more math, planning, and art), write labels for exhibit items and a short brochure for the entire exhibit (writing), and so on. PBL crosses discipline boundaries and gets students to look carefully at what they know, what they need to know, what actions they can take to solve the problem, and what alternate solutions might work.

PBL can work with state standards, or it can be used several times during the year as a method to promote critical thinking and creativity within an existing school curriculum. "In the problem-based learn-ing approach students are presented with an ill-structured problem and work in small groups to arrive at some resolution to the problem. The teacher is no longer the focus of all that happens, although the teacher plays a crucial role in selecting the problem and facilitating the student groups" (Ann Lambros, *Problem-Based Learning in K–8 Classrooms:* Corwin Press, 2002, vii). During a PBL unit, the teacher is always an active and involved participant in the entire learning process.

The role of the teacher in PBL varies from problem to problem. The teacher usually selects the problem, although this can be done jointly with older students, and collects some of the required material—depending on the age of the students—that will be needed to find pos-sible solutions. The teacher always works with the various groups that have been established to focus on all or parts of the problem, and the teacher sets up and usually participates in the method by which the pos-sible solutions will be judged.

Problems and possible solutions in PBL can be relatively simple or extremely complex, but the steps are roughly the same:

1. Present the problem: In six weeks, four new students from India will join our fourth-grade class. These students are Hindu, speak good English, but have never been to the United States. What can we do to make them feel comfortable and to show them that we know something about their culture?
2. Brainstorm ideas about how the problem could be "solved."
3. Collect all the facts, data, and information needed to get started.
4. List what the class needs to know and what the learning issues are.
5. Devise one or more specific action plans that might resolve the problem. Note: The class may be divided into three or four groups to do this.
6. Present conclusions reached based on the study and research un-dertaken.
7. Determine which conclusion or conclusions will best address the initial problem.
8. Take action.

Multiple Intelligences (MI)

MI has been in currency since 1983 when Howard Gardner published *Frames of Mind: The Theory of Multiple Intelligences* (New York, Basic Books) and presented considerable research that IQ was far too narrow a measure of intelligence. He cogently made the case that intelligence had to do with the ability to solve problems anywhere from a dance class to a science lab or to create products in settings that were natural and contained the necessary materials to create those products. To date, Gardner has suggested that there may be as many as nine basic intelligences ranging from the logical-mathematical intelligence used by, say, accountants and computer programmers in their work to interpersonal intelligence used by many politicians and other leaders to persuade people to support their proposals or themselves.

Gardner has made a case for linguistic intelligence, logical-mathematical intelligence, spatial intelligence, bodily kinesthetic intelligence, musical intelligence, interpersonal intelligence, intrapersonal intelligence, naturalist intelligence and is accumulating considerable evidence to make the case for existential intelligence, a form of spiritual-moral intelligence exemplified by such people as Nelson Mandela or Martin Luther King Jr. Thomas Armstrong in his best-selling book *Multiple Intelligences in the Classroom* (2nd edition, ASCD, 2000), makes the case for allowing students to find ways to express themselves through each of the intelligences, rather than limiting them to the two (linguistic and logical-mathematical) that have been the basis for work in most schools for more than one hundred years. Armstrong believes that each person possesses each of the intelligences to some degree, that most people can develop each intelligence to the point of competency, that the intelligences work together, and that there are many ways to be intelligent within each intelligence category.

The basic argument here is that students should be encouraged and helped to develop the intelligences in which they have natural and particular strengths and that schools should recognize the various intelligences as co-equal. While we should demand that every student read and write and compute well, we should also give full credit and opportunity to students who can best express their intelligence through verbal presentation or artistic expression or some other legitimate means. Schools that support MI approaches often have students learn some math through a building project; a serious art presentation could portray an historic event or the theme of a short story. Students often exhibit mature and carefully crafted charts or media presentations to get at complex science subjects; performances are used to interpret novels or important historical events.

9

WHAT ARE CONSTRUCTIVISM AND CONTENT-RICH CURRICULUM?

DISCUSSION

Constructivism and content-rich curriculum are often thought to be in opposition, but I don't agree with that, so I have yoked them together in the same question.

Constructivism has enormous implications for how a teacher runs a classroom and how curriculum is crafted. Constructivism is a theory of knowledge positing that students learn best through concrete experience, dialogue, active learning, and careful reflection; in effect, students are presented with information, a problem or an issue and resolve their cognitive conflicts by exploring that material until they have arrived at a satisfactory conclusion.

If the question before the class is "What holds an airplane up?" the teacher encourages a discussion of what the students will need to know to figure that out. The teacher becomes an active force in helping students organize their thinking and locating the information necessary to answer the question. With the teacher's help and guidance, the students are at the center of their own learning. Advocates of constructivism often say that "rigid" information-based curricula do little to help students learn in any deep way—they just master discrete pieces of information.

Content-rich curriculum advocates argue that students should learn a very rich body of information in common and that this body of information will be the basis for additional learning. The content-rich adherents want students to master a substantial sequence of information, particularly in grades K–8, that will be the basis for more sophisticated learning in later grades and college. They argue that education by objectives in early grades leaves students with huge curriculum gaps, particularly harming disadvantaged students who are not likely to get the information they need from an educationally stimulating home environment. Content-rich curriculum advocates often dismiss constructivism as a technique for approaching arbitrary problems or pieces of information. They argue that such an approach provides students with no systematic learning that can be built on from grade to grade.

The chief drum major for content-rich curriculum is E. D. Hirsch Jr. author of *Cultural Literacy: What Every American Needs to Know* (Houghton Mifflin, 1987) and *The Schools We Need and Why We Don't Have Them* (Doubleday, 1996). Professor Hirsch is also the founder of the Core Knowledge Foundation, which produces curriculum materials for the early grades. Timm Mackley, an Ohio superintendent of schools wrote a very helpful book on getting a content-rich curriculum into schools: *Uncommon Sense: Core Knowledge in the Classroom* (ASCD, 1999).

Martin Brooks and Jacqueline Grennon Brooks are the primary advocates of constructivism: *In Search of Understanding: The Case for Constructivist Classrooms* (ASCD, 1993 and 1999). Their book is one of the best-selling works in the history of ASCD. They have done workshops for thousands of teachers and administrators who find that constructivism can be combined with virtually any other method or curriculum. Another very helpful book on constructivism is *Who Will Save Our Schools? Teachers As Constructivist Leaders*, Linda Lambert et al. (Corwin Press, Inc., 1997).

PERSPECTIVE AND DETAILS

Since constructivism is a learning theory and content-rich curriculum is a body of information, there should be no conflict between the two, although too often educators who identify themselves as progressives take information-based curriculum lightly, and those who see themselves as conservatives dismiss constructivism as just another soft approach. My point is that you cannot have a curriculum without content, but having a curriculum that is all content and no exploration (critical thinking, problem solving, reflection) makes little sense either.

Constructivism, no matter what the curriculum, encourages students to approach learning by forming their own theories about concepts or information and includes such characteristics as the following:

1. Mistakes are often the basis for learning. Teachers can use misconceptions to help students figure out more accurately what is going on.
2. Students will need time and interaction with each other and the teacher to gain understanding.
3. More often than not, the teacher will use primary sources, raw data, or physical materials for lessons.
4. Most lessons will be structured around problems, questions, or situations that may not have one correct answer—very similar to problem-based learning.
5. Student reflection, group discussion, and all other forms of student thinking and interaction will be important in teaching.

Of course, lessons will have considerable content; students will look up or discover information and will need to master any content necessary to understand the lesson concept. You cannot take up questions about a work of literature or the Civil War or a science concept without mastering a great deal of information about those things.

Content-rich curriculum will be rooted in a carefully crafted sequence of information that will be presented from grades K–8. Schools that prefer this method of organizing study want to be certain that students learn a particular body of knowledge and that there is not repetition from grade-to-grade unless that is consciously desired for some important reason. Educators who favor content-rich curriculum do not want to see general statements about skills or even general statements about curriculum content. They want to see specific lists: first grade literature—*Hansel and Gretel, Jack and the Beanstalk, Pinocchio, How Anasi Got Stories from the Sky God,* and so on. They want to know that in a particular grade students will study the solar system, cell division, sound waves, and a half a dozen other specific science topics. In short, they want to be certain that students come out of the curriculum "culturally literate."

Schools or school districts may gather textbooks and other materials and form their own curriculum, a substantial but very engaging enterprise, or they may simply purchase materials from a commercial publisher or nonprofit organization such as the Core Knowledge Foundation. Obviously, if a school district can afford to bring teachers together to create a content-rich curriculum, the teachers will have a greater stake in the curriculum than if it is simply purchased.

It seems to me that school districts, depending on their philosophical bent, can determine that a content-rich or constructivist approach should be dominant. If the former, there is no reason why the content-rich materials cannot be the basis for a constructivist approach—at least some of the time. If the latter, the constructivist teachers can follow at least some of the content-rich curriculum for their lessons. Studying a work of literature or a science concept should include both mastery of information as well as discovery of methods to analyze or classify or speculate about or make predictions based on whatever is under study.

The process-content debate has been going on for several decades. It should not be an either/or debate; rather, individual school districts need to determine only which dominance makes them more comfortable. Theoretically, of course, there can be a balance, but I have not yet seen a district where one dominance or the other is not preferred.

10

WHAT ARE TEACHER PORTFOLIOS?

DISCUSSION

Teacher portfolios are relatively new—at least in the sense that their use in the past ten or fifteen years is now coming into more common practice. Simply stated, teacher portfolios are a collection of materials that illustrate to the teacher what some of his or her strengths and weaknesses are, that help the teacher to reflect on his or her practice, and that may be used, if the teacher grants permission or chooses, to help colleagues, administrators, certification agencies, or prospective employers evaluate that teacher—for anything from growth to certification to hiring and tenure.

More and more, school districts are asking teacher candidates to submit a modest portfolio as part of the teacher's application. This may include a video excerpt from previous teaching or student teaching and some short statements on educational beliefs and preferred practices. Many districts now recommend or require that new teachers keep a portfolio as part of the evaluation process that will lead to permanent employment. Each district has its own list of what the teacher may or must include in the portfolio. The National Board for Professional Teaching Standards (NBPTS) uses teacher portfolios as part of its program for granting national certification. Many school districts regard the NBPTS's demanding process to certification as prestigious and subsidize the costs to the teacher, grant additional salary to successful candidates—or both.

PERSPECTIVE AND DETAILS

Teacher portfolios can have any of dozens of things in them including but not limited to the items listed below. The important thing to remember is that the portfolio is not a dead file or collection. It is ever-changing as the teacher's point of view, needs, repertoire, and other characteristics of a rounded, evolving teacher change. The third-year teacher is a very different professional from the first-year teacher—and that will be reflected in what the teacher eliminates from or inserts in the portfolio. In fact, the teacher may move from third grade to first grade or vice versa or may add a language or another science to his or her repertoire in a secondary school. Of course, some items may remain in the portfolio to give the teacher a history of growth.

- Videotapes of the teacher in the classroom. There may be a variety of short tapes (5 to 20 minutes) illustrating the different kinds of teaching this person does. A teacher may wish to show excerpts from anything from lecture to lecture-discussion, cooperative groups, or a one-to-one conference with a student.
- Samples of student work. Depending on the grade and subject, this could include art work, essays, math work, photographs of such student work as models or science fair exhibitions, or short tapes of student presentations, performances, or exhibitions.
- Philosophy of teaching. The teacher would probably write a short statement of strongest beliefs about how he or she plans to teach and help students learn and grow. This statement will undergo constant change as the teacher becomes more experienced, learns new approaches, and is influenced by other teachers or professional development courses.
- Professional journal. Many teachers keep a professional journal, particularly during the first three years of teaching. The journal entries could be daily, but more often they are weekly—perhaps a fif-

teen or twenty-minute entry each Friday afternoon. Here the teacher tries to capture some of the highlights of the week. Some teachers just write about their experiences; others like a more structured approach and have sections titled, for instance, Best Practice of Week, Worst Practice of Week, Highlight Event of Week.

Note: This is a good time to pause—since some teacher-readers may be getting slightly nervous—to emphasize that the teacher is fully in charge of the portfolio. Not many second-year teachers would care to write that the highlight event of the week was an unsatisfying conversation with the assistant principal for whom he or she has less respect each week but who will examine the teacher's portfolio and write a final evaluation. If the portfolio is for the teacher's reflection and sharing with a group of other untenured teachers and an outside expert who does not share the content with administrators, the teacher will write more freely than if the supervising administrator is going to have access to every part of the portfolio.

The teacher must always determine what to put in the portfolio and what to share with whom. Some teachers keep a required portfolio and then have some additional materials they use for their own reflection or sharing with a few trusted colleagues. In other cases, the administration and the teachers agree on what the supervisors will see and what is optional. Back to the list:

- Videotapes or other records to illustrate work outside the classroom. Here the teacher may have some material that illustrates his or her work with parents, an administrator or a committee the teacher has chosen to join. Some teachers take on additional responsibilities such as coaching or club leadership and wish to collect material that illustrates this. This can be journal entries, photographs, testimonial letters from others, excerpts from longer videotapes, or anything else that captures what the teacher has done.
- Detailed record of a particular unit. A teacher may do a problem-based learning unit that takes two weeks, or there might be a required unit of similar length in the district's curriculum that is recorded in some detail. Because of the detail, this is something the

teacher might do just once each year. Many of the items above would be included here, but there might also be a rubric or some other assessment tool that would aid the teacher and others in evaluating what took place and how successful it was.

- Diagnosis of student learning. This could include evidence that a teacher has used several forms of assessment, from teacher-created short tests of all sorts to individual conferences to state tests, to determine how to help a student, a group, or an entire class.
- Analysis of materials. This section would demonstrate that, when choice is possible, the teacher has looked at classroom materials, textbooks, laboratory equipment, art supplies, and the like and made informed decisions about what to use or recommend for purchase. This could, of course, reflect a decision made as part of a committee.

Many districts organize the accumulation of a teacher portfolio around a study group or professional development course. This is very helpful in that it gives some structure, regularity, and support to the effort. Author Giselle Martin-Kniep summarizes the possibilities for portfolio creation in her excellent and practical book on the subject: "Professional portfolios can be developed in a variety of contexts including in-service programs, collegial circles, or as part of the evaluation/supervision process. They can be developed through a formal and directed process (the portfolio developer is told what to include and annotate) or in a self-directed and informal process (the portfolio developer identifies the kinds of work that ought to be included and reflects on the work as the opportunity arises)" (*Capturing the Wisdom of Practice: Professional Portfolios for Educators*, ASCD, 1999, pp. 3–4).

In a typical study group or collegial circle, six to fifteen people gather, perhaps once each month for three hours, to share their portfolios, to talk about progress in the classroom, to help each other reflect on what is in the portfolios and possible steps to improvement, to discuss how they accumulated material, and to talk about more effective or efficient ways to gather appropriate materials. Often, the study group is led by a very experienced teacher who will not be reporting back to any supervisor of these teachers—other than to present a record of attendance and work completed.

Again, some school districts now require portfolios for pre-service and nontenured teachers, but increasingly districts are using portfolios to help experienced teachers self-evaluate their performance and to renew their teaching. Virtually everyone is learning that teachers make the most progress when the portfolios can be completely honest. This means that everyone knows at the outset which parts of the portfolio are open to administrative inspection and which are not.

11

WHAT IS THE BEST WAY
TO EDUCATE LIMITED ENGLISH
PROFICIENT (LEP) STUDENTS?

DISCUSSION

The issue here is about how "bilingual education" should be conducted. There are no villains in this discussion, only people who wish to help non- or limited-users of English learn how to use the language well enough to function in the culture, to gain reasonable employment, and to go on to higher education, if that is what an individual desires. The essential debate today is between the advocates of traditional bilingual education and those who favor Structured English Immersion (SEI).

PERSPECTIVE AND DETAILS

The first thing to know is that this is not a small or inconsequential matter. According to Johanna Haver (*Structured English Immersion: An Approach that Works*, Corwin Press, Inc., 2002), there are well over four million LEP students in our schools and that population is growing far more rapidly than the general school population. About 73 percent of those students are Spanish speakers, and the remaining 27 percent are distributed among more than one hundred language and ethnic groups. Harold Hodgkinson, a leading educational demographer, said in an Education Life section interview in the *New York Times* ("Q & A," Karen W. Arenson, August 5, 2001, p. 14) that "the No. 1 demographic change is probably the increase in ethnic diversity in America. If you look 20 years out, 63 percent of the new population growth in the United States will be Spanish and Asian." This, of course, continues the trend of the past twenty years.

The year 2000 census revealed that "nearly 1 in 5 Americans does not speak English at home. . . . Not only are more U.S. residents reporting that they do not speak English at home, more than 10.5 million said they speak little or no English. That is up from 6.5 million in 1990" (D'Vera Cohn and Sarah Cohen, *Washington Post*, August 6, 2001, p. A1).

While it is true that six states—California, Texas, New York, Florida, Illinois, and Arizona—account for about 60 percent of the nation's LEP students, and in that rank order of magnitude, Georgia has twenty-two thousand students, North Carolina has twenty-nine thousand, and South Dakota has nearly eight thousand LEP students. In the small Georgia town of East Point, just a few miles south of Atlanta, several hundred Mexicans and Mexican Americans work in local businesses. Virtually all of the immigrants are from one small farming town in Mexico named Ejido Modelo, about two hundred miles west and north of Mexico City, that has fallen on hard times. First a few men, and then later their families and neighbors, began the migration in 1984 to find good jobs and low rents. It is not possible to say with precision how many Mexicans are in this town, because of the many hundreds of immigrants some are there legally and others are not.

This migration story has been repeated all over the United States and is the reason why there is a federal proposal to consider granting some form of permanent status to millions of recent immigrants who are, for the most part, gainfully employed and not likely to return to their original homes in Mexico, Vietnam, or elsewhere except for brief visits.

All of the figures cited derive from the 2000 census numbers used by the U.S. Department of Education or other substantial and respected government agencies. It is very difficult to get a handle on absolutely accurate figures because, again, some of the immigrants are not here legally and others move one or more times during each year. What is clear is that most of the adults are employed, they are virtual residents of the United States, and their children are in our schools. These children are in schools in each of our fifty states, and teaching them good English is clearly in the national interest.

According to Peter Duignan's summary of research done for the Hoover Institution at Stanford University (www-hoover.stanford. edu/publication/he/22/22a.html), bilingual education traces back to the Civil Rights Act of 1964 and the Bilingual Education Act of 1968. The original intention was that "a child should be instructed in his or her native tongue for a transitional year while she or he learned English but was to transfer to an all-English classroom as fast as possible" (p. 1). This, however, is not what happened in most places. Bilingual education continued beyond the first year, and many Spanish speakers, for instance, remained "in classrooms where essentially Spanish was taught, and bilingual education became Spanish cultural maintenance with English limited to thirty minutes a day," again according to Peter Duignan (p. 1). The situation may be more complicated than this, but the important point is that in many places bilingual education has extended far beyond a year or two, and many students never master English.

While both local and federal funding have increased very substantially for LEP students—perhaps to more than ten billion dollars annually—achievement gains have been unsatisfactory. Haver states in her book that the dropout rate for Hispanics "has fluctuated between 25% and 35% from 1972 to 1997. In 1998, 30 percent of Hispanic 16- to 24-year-olds were dropouts, versus 14 percent of blacks and 8 percent of whites" (forthcoming). Most of the statistical information available is on Hispanics since they are by far the largest group (73 percent) in LEP programs. Each of the other groups is very small, with only the Vietnamese rising to 4 percent of the LEP population and the majority of the many other groups constituting far less than 1 percent.

Again, there are no villains here, but there is growing criticism of bilingual programs as they are practiced in many places. In the past five years, two states, Arizona and California, have passed propositions that have brought about changes in how LEP children will be taught. In both states, school districts are now required to offer Structured English Immersion (SEI) courses during a transition period not to exceed one year. There is no effort here, according to adherents of these propositions, to undermine anyone's native culture, but there is a clear effort under these propositions to do everything possible to improve the English skills of these children, particularly elementary age children, to the point where they can take demanding high school courses, get good jobs, or go to college.

Around the country, there is lively interest in the SEI approach from Colorado to New York City. Many of the SEI practices are similar to excellent practices that have been used in bilingual programs for years. It is important to remember that "SEI is not necessarily an all-English program, but it does make considerably less use of the non-English language for instruction than does bilingual education" (Keith Baker, Phi Delta *Kappan*, November 1998, p. 7, PDK Home version online).

A hero in this effort to educate non-native speakers is Jaime Escalante whose success with Hispanic students was depicted in the 1988 movie *Stand and Deliver*, a semi-documentary recounting of his work with relatively poor Latino high school students in Los Angeles who passed the Advanced Placement (AP) Calculus Exam. Escalante is not a supporter of traditional bilingual education, but believes these children, while remaining proud of their native heritage and retaining their native language, need to master English as quickly as possible to do well in the majority culture. SEI emphasizes the use of English in highly structured lessons that lead the student to use some English soon after instruction begins—in some cases within hours, days, or, at most, a week or two. Students are combined with or moved into mainstream classes at the earliest reasonable moment—meaning as soon as they are ready to perform competently and eventually do well there.

Again, students in SEI classes use many of the techniques practiced in traditional bilingual settings. The chief differences are that there is more emphasis on English right from the start, that students know this is a transitional period of a few months to a year for virtually all of them, and that the teacher will combine these students with mainstream classes as soon and as often as possible. Traditional bilingual adherents argue that getting students on a sound footing in all subjects in their native language will lead to greater achievement in all-English instruction when the students are ready for that—even if it takes an extra year or two or more. They are also very concerned about the retention of excellent native language skills and devotion to the native culture.

Bilingual learning is one of the many difficult issues in education that have no clear answer and that have both pedagogical and political concerns built into them. For those who believe the key to success in American culture is English, SEI may be more effective, and early results from California seem to bear that out. Haver, citing statistics published in the *New York Times*, states that "Two years after the passing of California's Proposition 227, reports appeared that LEP students had improved in all subjects due to the elimination of bilingual education and the implementation of structured immersion." Haver goes on to say that the Research in English Acquisition and Development (READ) Institute "concluded that the greatest gains were made in school districts that chose the strictest interpretation of the initiative and implemented the most intensive English-immersion programs" (Haver, Corwin Press, Inc., forthcoming).

Of course, such results are not uncommon in the early stages of new programs. It remains to be seen what happens to the native language, to reverence for the native culture, and to language acquisition results over time as SEI takes hold and as the inevitable changes occur in places that continue to practice more traditional bilingual education, but respond to some of the criticism of the slowness of the programs.

What is becoming undeniable is that educators, parents, and many politicians and community members want LEP students to move to good or excellent English use more rapidly than has been the case in the past. It is the combination of solid English skills, pride in one's heritage, and good skills in one's native language that produces success.

12

WHAT DO I NEED TO
KNOW ABOUT RUBRICS?

DISCUSSION

Rubrics are now used widely in schools, but perhaps not widely enough. Simply stated, "A rubric is a scoring tool that lists the criteria for a piece of work, or 'what counts' (for example, purpose, organization, details, voice, and mechanics are often what counts in a piece of writing); it also articulates gradations of quality for each criterion, from excellent to poor" (Heidi Goodrich Andrade, "Understanding Rubrics," *Educational Leadership*, December/January 1997, www.middleweb. com/rubricsHG.html). The rubric lists all the elements, or at least the most important elements, in a particular type of writing, lab experiment, oral presentation, drawing, or any other student work as well as tells the student what constitutes different levels of quality.

To make this graphic, table 12.1 is a rubric for this book. If you accept this rubric as accurate, it gives you a way to judge my book. If this were a classroom, I probably would have handed this to you before you started the book, so you could determine by question 3 or 4 if this was worthwhile reading for you. Of course, you might want to include other or additional criteria for judging my book.

Table 12.1.   Rubric for this Book

	Gradations of Quality			
Criteria	Minimally Acceptable: 1	Acceptable: 2	Above Expectations: 3	Outstanding: 4
Readability	Not at an appropriate level; too much jargon and unclear	Level is good; most of the text is clear	Level was just right; text very clear	Absolutely correct level; text extremely clear; almost no problems with readability
Applicability	Very few questions applied to me; most of the questions were not germane	At least half of the questions interested me; many questions were right on target	Most of the questions interested me; all of the questions were relevant	All of the questions interested me; everything was extremely germane
Helpfulness	Almost nothing I could use; very removed from my situation; poor questions, discussion, recommendations, and examples	Enough applied to me to make the book worthwhile; some of the questions, recommendations, and discussion were useful to me	Most of the questions applied to me; most of the discussion and recommendations were interesting and useful to me	All of the questions were of great interest; almost all of the discussion and recommendations will help in my work

DISCUSSION AND DETAILS

The rubric I have supplied is rather simple. Rubrics can be even sim-
pler, or they can be far more complex. I could have supplied a fourth or
fifth category in the Criteria column; I could have limited the Gradations of Quality to three levels, or I could have added a fifth level of
quality. I could have limited my quality descriptions to one or two
words, or I could have made them even more detailed—perhaps several
sentences each. Basically, what this and other rubrics do "is to make an
essentially subjective process as clear, consistent, and defensible as possible" (Judith Arter and Jay McTighe, *Scoring Rubrics in the Classroom*,
Corwin Press, Inc., 2001, p. 5). There is no mathematically certain way
to say my book is better or worse than X's book or better or worse than
most readers had a right to expect, but you can construct meaningful
categories that make the judgment far more precise and considerably

more supportable than just rendering an opinion based on no carefully-wrought criteria.

Accurate, effective rubrics are not easy to construct, and many teachers find that after using the rubric, they must make some changes. For instance, you construct a rubric on a piece of writing or an oral presentation—but then two third- or tenth-grade students write a composition or make a presentation that is better than and different from what you anticipated. You acknowledge their outstanding work and change the rubric. By trial and error, teachers soon learn to construct very useful rubrics. There are several other ways to create rubrics, some more efficient and others very demanding, that will lead to excellent rubrics for classroom use. There are even methods for anticipating problems like the one above.

Teams of teachers can work together on rubrics of common interest. Four eighth-grade math teachers constructing a rubric for use at the end of a two-week unit are far more likely to create the four or five or six best criteria for judging that unit as well as precise quality gradations than one teacher working alone.

The best way to construct a rubric is to have student work in front of you. This is an excellent use of teacher workshop time if it is available in your district. Assume that three fifth-grade teachers working together have the project materials from a science unit they each did on what could be found in a local pond. None of the teachers used rubrics in their classroom, but they just had a several-hour workshop on rubrics and would like to use this technique next year.

The first step is to look at the project materials and the grades they gave them and sort them into groups—perhaps four groups ranging from the poorest projects to the best. Since the teachers graded the project materials using traditional scoring, the sorting should not take too long. Now the teachers quickly eliminate the projects where they can't agree on the sort and are soon left with, perhaps, five to seven examples in each of the four categories.

The next step is to start discussing what makes the best examples so good. It is always a good idea to start with the best student examples and work back; this gives you an accurate picture of what the most successful students can do—in effect, models of excellence. Looking carefully at actual student work allows you to create very accurate and helpful criteria and quality categories. This technique is time consuming, but it is an outstanding way to get teachers talking to each other about quality and results in thorough and excellent rubrics.

Teams of teachers, usually small groups of three to five, can often create three to five excellent rubrics in a single workshop day, once they have some training and experience. More complex rubrics, often based on a long unit or a type of instruction that will recur, require more teacher discussion and more trial and error and may take a team an entire day to complete. If rubrics appeal to you, set aside planning time for small groups of teachers to work together at regular intervals. The bonus here is that this gets teachers talking about quality and curriculum at regular meetings throughout the school year.

Rubrics can be used for any instruction—no exceptions. However, teachers probably should not use rubrics all of the time. First, as already said, they take time to construct. Second, they are most useful when used with moderately to fairly complex instruction—often that means a unit of some sort. For instance, if you are doing a two-week science or interdisciplinary project or a writing project that begins with gathering material, goes through revisions and culminates in a short paper or essay, a rubric is a good idea.

Students can learn to construct very simple rubrics and can be included in a discussion of what should be in a rubric. This gets young people thinking about goals and quality.

Many teachers give students the rubric as a way of beginning a discussion of what the class is about to undertake. This takes the mystery out of grading and shows students what they must accomplish to qualify for a high rating.

Rubrics can include both quality and quantity. In a seventh grade social studies unit on elections, to qualify for the highest rating students might see on the rubric that they need to use at least five written sources and two interviews with adults who have voted in a national election, that they need to use at least five newspaper or magazine articles, and that their final oral presentation must include examples of problems or issues from at least three different states or types of elections. Of course, there will be many indicators of quality on the rubric as well.

In her helpful book, *Becoming a Better Teacher: Eight Innovations That Work* (ASCD, 2000), Giselle Martin-Kniep devotes a chapter to rubrics and makes two important points that must be added to what I've said above. First, rubrics are "a critical component of authentic assessment tasks" (p. 34), and schools are increasingly using problem-based learning and sophisticated tasks with real consequences for instruction. Students determine water quality in a local pond or stream, they write letters to mayors and commissioners about community issues they've researched, and they help to design play areas or create art work for their schools. These tasks are best evaluated by rubrics, which Martin-Kniep says can identify "all the needed attributes of quality or development in a process, product, or performance" (p. 34).

Second, Martin-Kniep points out that rubrics can be holistic or analytic. A holistic rubric assigns a single score to an entire product, process, or performance. A holistic rubric for a social studies essay in the ninth grade would simply list five or six levels of performance from excellent to poor and one level would be assigned as an assessment to the student's essay (or portfolio of work with additional indicators in the rubric to reflect preliminary stages.)

A level 5 essay (highest rating) on persuading the board of education to construct a new soccer field at the school might read as follows:

- presents case very forcefully and clearly at or near the beginning of essay;
- uses some clear principle of organization;
- makes very few technical errors;
- uses at least four effective examples of need to support position;
- anticipates problems the board could raise.

A level 1 essay (lowest rating) might state the following:

- presents case vaguely at the outset;
- uses no clear principle of organization;
- makes many technical errors;
- uses only one or two examples and they are not clear or appropriate;
- anticipates none of board's needs or problems.

An analytic rubric would look like the one I supplied for this book. There would be separate categories for each criterion, and a student could score differently on each one. A science project rubric could get the highest rating for the use of charts, slides, and other visual aids; a medium rating for the student's oral presentation; but a fairly high rating for the two-page written summary of the project.

Rubrics for very simple tasks can be created by a teacher who has some experience with them in about thirty minutes. More complex rubrics can take an hour or two, and rubrics that involve very careful team instruction can take at least several hours, and sometimes a day or two. Rubrics can help with everything from preparing students for a unit to assessments of all kinds to teacher discussions of curriculum and quality. Many states use rubrics to gauge their standards and encourage teachers to construct and use rubrics when preparing students for instruction and eventually the state tests. Martin-Kniep has found that constructing classroom rubrics works very well with state standards, allowing teachers to think through what they need to do with students and how they should judge student accomplishment against the standards and the material that will be assessed on state examinations.

IV

LARGE ISSUES: SAFETY, LEADERSHIP, AND QUALITY TEACHERS

This part examines the following questions.

Question 13: What will be required to keep schools safe?
Question 14: What are some characteristics of leadership in education?
Questions 15: What needs to be done to ensure a quality teaching force in 2015?

If our schools are safe, if our teachers and administrators exhibit qualities of real leadership, and if the schools are staffed by highly skilled and motivated teachers, many of the difficulties raised in critically constructive reports on education will have been alleviated by 2015. This is a complicated business, and "if" is a very big word in spite of having only two letters.

This part examines three very important questions and tries to bring them down to earth. Schools can be made far safer, but some of the proposals and criticisms suggested by politicians and other lay people won't work or are expensive beyond anything close to reality or need. There are, however, things that will work and cost relatively little. Leadership has always been required in schools and everywhere else. We know that leadership must be several things simultaneously: concentrated in a few "natural" positional leaders such as principals, delegated to several supervisors, and distributed in significant ways to teachers if anything is to be done. The president of our country, for instance, can and should be a strong leader, but without his cabinet, the congress, the military, the courts, other parts of the government, the business community, the schools, and the general populace, he cannot do very much.

Several books and articles have been and will be written on replacing at least two million teachers and administrators between now and 2015. Each year now, 150,000 to 275,000 teachers and administrators born between 1945 and 1955 will complete thirty or more years of service and choose to retire. An additional 30,000 or more educators will simply leave the profession each year—often to enter a profession where salaries are higher. This is the largest opportunity we've ever had in American education to consider how we should go about recruiting and inducting people of very high quality into the profession. We all know how central the teacher is to student and school success, and we know the vital role that administrators play—particularly school principals. Virtually every school district in the nation must consider the question of how to go about this recruitment-retention process in a way that will benefit their school community for decades to come.

⑬

WHAT WILL BE REQUIRED
TO KEEP SCHOOLS SAFE?

DISCUSSION

In light of recent tragic events in places such as Littleton, Colorado, (Columbine High School) and more than a dozen other schools since 1993 from Paducah, Kentucky, to Jonesboro, Arkansas, and Moses Lake, Washington—not to mention several credible threats that have been thwarted such as one in New Bedford, Massachusetts, in late 2001—a great deal of media attention has been focused on keeping schools safe. Some people believe we should have police or other guards in every school; others have suggested metal detectors at each school door; of course, zero tolerance has been proposed as a school policy in many places.

PERSPECTIVE AND DETAILS

We need to gain some distance here. According to a *New York Times* article by John Leland on April 8, 2001, the "Juvenile Law Center, a nonprofit organization in Philadelphia, noted that students are three times as likely to be hit by lightning as to be killed by violence in schools" (p. 1).

While it is a fact that schools are among the safest places in our society,
it is clearly not a good idea to be complacent about risks to children, but
it is also not a good idea to overreact to imagined risks or to supply expensive protection where it is not needed or won't work.

- Putting metal detectors and guards at every school door would be
  wildly expensive and might not help. Most schools (because of fire
  safety laws) have twenty to forty doors. Will we guard each one?
- Teenagers, particularly in buildings with low windows, and most
  schools have dozens of those, can find many ways to get contra-
  band, weapons, and even themselves into school buildings against
  our wishes. An angry, resourceful teenager is very hard to stop unless you know in advance he or she is angry and about to explode.
- Zero tolerance only works when it is applied intelligently and judi-
  ciously. Anne Gearan of the Associated Press in a February 14,
  2001, release reported that a Pittsburgh kindergartner was disci-
  plined in 1999 "because his Halloween firefighter costume contained a plastic ax." In Cobb County, Georgia, Gearan writes, a
  sixth grader was suspended in 2000 "because the 10-inch key chain
  on her Tweety bird wallet is considered a weapon." Russ Kiba and
  Reece Peterson published a table of very questionable applications
  of zero tolerance policies in a January, 1999, Phi Delta *Kappan* article. They cited a six-year-old in Colorado Springs who shared
  organic lemon drops with students on the playground and was suspended for possession of "other chemical substances." In Colum-
  bus, Ohio, according to Kiba and Peterson, a nine-year-old was suspended for one day before actually arriving in the school because
  the child had a manicure kit with a one-inch "knife." Such actions
  do nothing to prevent violence, but everything to make school officials look foolish.
- The attack on the World Trade Center and the Pentagon on September 11, 2001, has justifiably made everyone wary of future ter-
  rorist attacks. We can only pray that schools will never be a target
  and that dramatically increased vigilance by every level of government and all citizens will thwart attacks, but there is no realistic
  way to provide sufficient barriers and firepower at every school (or

church or synagogue or business location or hospital or any place other than military bases and a selected number of other likely targets) to resist misguided, heavily armed adult terrorists on a suicide mission. Schools must be alert, but, again, it is increased vigilance at every level that is our strongest safeguard.

So what can be done to make schools much safer from angry young people about to explode into violence, recognizing that no program or combination of programs can make any school or stadium or shopping mall or post office or any other place 100 percent safe, but that steps can and should be taken to make schools safer?

- Make the school far more personal. Dividing large schools into smaller schools will help. This does not mean building new buildings or adding expense. You can have two or three smaller schools inside one building. Every aspect of discipline and contact improves when the staff and the students know each other. Adult staff and students will notice and report highly unusual or frightening behavior in an intimate setting. The high road to learning which student might represent a credible threat to a school is to create a personalized atmosphere where students feel comfortable talking to staff and staff members notice changes in student behavior. Don't underestimate the ability of a school aide or custodian in a small setting to spot a student in difficulty. Remember, at least 99 out of 100 times when a student is in difficulty, all that is required is some conversation with an adult, some parental intervention, a referral to a guidance counselor or the school psychologists. Most schools will never experience, or even come close to, the tragedy at Columbine and other places.
- Use an advisory system in secondary schools; most serious school violence occurs in grades 6 through 12. The advisory system is one in which every student is assigned an adult advisor. By using every professional in the building (principal, librarian, psychologist, guidance counselor), most schools can bring the ratio down to approximately 1:15. There are many variations on the advisory program, but the point is that every student has an adult advisor with whom

she or he has fairly regular contact, perhaps even daily contact in a small group for a few minutes, and who has special responsibility for that student. The advisor is alert to changes in the student's behavior or attitude and has some contact, in most advisory systems, with the student's family. Again, this personalizes the school. I have a self-serving, but sincere and legitimate, interest here, since I wrote the book on advisory: *How to Design an Advisory System for a Secondary School* (ASCD, 1998).

- Use cooperative learning techniques occasionally in classroom instruction where it is logical and natural. There is considerable research to support using this technique for pedagogical reasons, but the bonus is that students come to know each other far better than they would in an impersonal class where virtually all the discussion and answers are directed at the teacher. When students work together in cooperative groups they are less likely to develop hostile feelings and more likely to appreciate each others' strengths.

- In some schools, having a police officer in or near the school may be a good idea. Practicing zero tolerance when it makes compelling sense (student claims to have a weapon or makes a credible threat), educating students, parents, and staff to report disturbing information immediately to some school authority, training many staff members to evaluate such information, working closely with police on what to do in the event of a threat or an incident, and taking many other steps can be helpful. However, and again, making your school a smaller, more personal place will do more to increase the chance of learning who, if anyone, is a threat to safety than any other technique I know.

- In cases where there is imminent danger to students (two teachers report John is roaming the halls with a seven-inch knife), obviously school action is taken at once to control John, the police are called and any safety plan the school has is put into action. In other cases, there should be a group of professionals (perhaps the principal, assistant principal, three designated teachers, psychologist, guidance counselor, social worker) who know they may be called on with no notice to evaluate a threat that is not imminent but needs attention within hours. The group should be large enough to ensure that at least three people will always be available. This group should practice with professionals, including police and school officials, who have experience with student threats.

- Every school should have a safety plan. Teachers, students, and administrators should know what to do in the event of a threatening situation. In elementary schools, the responsibility will be primarily on teachers for immediate action in the classroom—simple measures such as where to take the children or how to keep track of the children. In secondary schools, the youngsters can be included, but no safety plan should be unduly frightening to students. Again, the teachers have a major role for doing the immediate, simple things to protect students. There should be a more detailed plan kept in several places in the building, and the principal and other people, perhaps all of the members of the safety group, should know where those plans are kept. If there is adequate warning, the plan is consulted to see if the six or eight possibilities in it apply and can effectively be brought into action.

  Each year, the safety plan should be reviewed at least once to make necessary changes and to maintain familiarity with the safety procedures. Under no conditions should this plan be filed away to collect dust—no matter how many years go by without serious incident. Someone in authority should be obligated to take responsibility for the annual reviews and to report to the board of education and the staff that the review has been completed.

- Finally, and again, keep in mind that the overwhelming majority of schools are extremely safe places and that while vigilance is important, there is no need to react as if every school is a war zone. Students exaggerate or say things in jest all the time. The responsible adults must evaluate these "threats" to safety and take none lightly, but they should not react to every loose student utterance as if that youngster is coming to school in a few hours with an arsenal.

If there is a report that Johnny or Mary has talked about getting revenge on some students and claims to have a gun, by all means school authorities, police, and parents should be notified immediately and an appropriate investigation begun immediately. Immediately does not mean in a day or two, but right away. On the other hand, if two students are clearly joking or speaking metaphorically about an event that will never happen ("I could kill Mary for what she said about me and John"), the student might be warned to use other language, but likely nothing stronger than that should be done.

This is a balancing effort where we must remember that every student life is precious, that we never want to make a mistake, and that we should always err on the side of caution. However, we do not want to turn our schools into armed camps or places where teenagers cannot speak in normal way. A dozen schools have experienced dreadful tragedies in the past ten years; tens of thousands of schools across the country have not.

WHAT ARE SOME CHARACTERISTICS OF LEADERSHIP IN EDUCATION?

DISCUSSION

The answer to this question of characteristics of leadership in education is very easy, and the answer indicates why there are so many leadership programs, articles, and books that head in somewhat different directions. And the answer is, whatever works responsibly, sensibly, and with great integrity in the circumstances of a particular school or district.

PERSPECTIVE AND DETAILS

Does this mean that there are no commonalities among leaders, that there are no guideposts at all? No, in fact, there are some guideposts; there just are no strict rules. In the research for my book *Lessons from Exceptional School Leaders* (ASCD, 2001), I did locate some commonalities among leaders.

Forming beliefs and pursuing excellence were often the first steps for a leader. This applied to forming a union (Al Shanker), creating a computer program (Seymour Papert), running a school (principals Dennis Littky or Debby Meier), or teaching writing to high school students (teachers Audre Allison and Florence Mondry) and dozens of other people I interviewed in person.

Looking around very carefully to see what is needed constitutes the first step toward forming beliefs. Usually this involves several staff members, since many things may be needed, but no school can do everything. What are our two highest priorities? Is it an improved reading program, a new science program, a block schedule, increased attention to minority students, cooperative learning, or something else? Each school and district must go through this process of establishing the very few priorities behind which it will put first belief and then energy, time, and resources.

Locating excellence is the next necessary ingredient in forming beliefs. Where are some outstanding reading programs that might fit our needs? Who has written an article or book about cooperative learning that might help us understand what to do? What schools in our area have science programs that are successful and might be right for our school? You are not looking for just any excellent program; you are looking for an excellent program that very likely will be a good fit for your school.

Recognize from day one that everything works under certain conditions listed below (See A to E below.), and this makes your selection work much harder—but more effective if done properly. When you look at Success for All or the National Writing Project or any one of several programs that feature multiple intelligences, Core Knowledge, constructivism or block scheduling, you will find that serious researchers have given these programs their imprimatur and that there will be considerable anecdotal evidence to support each program.

CHARACTERISTICS OF EFFECTIVE PROGRAMS

A. The program is substantial. It is based on theory, research, and practice. The National Writing Project is a good example here— one of the largest and most successful programs available.

B. The program is well crafted. There are guidelines, materials, pamphlets, books, videos, CD-ROMs, and other carefully produced aids that establish parameters and give you choices. In many cases, teachers in a school or district have written their own materials based on other programs and existing materials, or they have adapted existing materials to fit their idiosyncratic needs. Most interesting programs require that teams of teachers work on them. It is beyond one teacher to do all the work required to prepare a program for a school. The Coalition of Essential Schools and Core Knowledge—very different from each other—are examples of well-crafted programs, although the former has more flexible guidelines than the latter.

C. The school or district is prepared to offer reasonable professional training to support the new program. Some programs require fifteen hours of training and others require two hundred hours spread over three years. Most programs worth doing are mature, sophisticated, and have some degree of complexity. They require rigorous training, and there is no way around that. More will be said about staff development below.

D. The principal is enthusiastic about the program, especially important in an elementary school. You can easily fill in the positions of other administrators in your school or district who need to be supportive of a program if it is to succeed. Much has been written about the role of administrators in the success of a school. There is no question but that leadership needs to be broadened, but there is also no question about the central role supportive administrators can play.

E. The program must have considerable staff support, and the word "considerable" means at least 70 percent of the staff is behind this program to some reasonable degree. Almost no school ever gets 100 percent support for anything—or even close to it. If you wait for every naysayer to get behind a new program or if you insist that the 70 percent be wildly enthusiastic, you will never start anything. Support for excellent programs will grow over time, but probably never exceed 80 or 85 percent of the staff. You must accept that.

Staff development is critical in any serious educational program. It is not enough to engage the staff's interest in cooperative learning or Core Knowledge curriculum or multiple intelligences. From John Goodlad to

Linda Darling-Hammond to Martin Brooks, educational leaders have emphasized rigorous training of teachers and administrators in excellent new methods or programs you wish to introduce to your school or district. Following are some guidelines for achieving an excellent program.

- Limit your staff development priorities. Perhaps three or four major efforts over four years is about right. This gives you focus.
- You need to devote time and money to staff development. Not every school district can afford to bring in national experts or pay teachers for long sessions in the summer. Within your district's ability, however, you must make some reasonable amount of time and money available for training. If your district's view is that training is a frill, you are lacking in district leadership and heading for mediocrity.
- People at the center of a particular staff development program should be supported to the greatest extent possible. Send them to conferences, give them petty cash for books and materials, allow them time and money to get training.
- Staff development must be a serious enterprise. All meetings should have an agenda. Workshop leaders should be qualified; they might be people on your own staff who have been trained by experts. There should be serious work: for instance, readings, practice or role-playing of techniques, thoughtful discussion, guest lectures, visits to places where similar programs are thriving. Staff development does not mean that people just get together to compare random notes.
- Provide incentives for teachers or administrators to take inservice courses. This can range from payment to inservice credit, from funds to attend conferences to funds for teaching materials. Some districts even have contractual agreements about staff development.
- Include the entire school community in staff development. Give progress reports on staff development at board meetings and parent meetings. Mention your programs in any district mailings or newsletter, whenever appropriate. Give your faculty updates at staff meetings. Ask your local (small community) newspaper or cable TV station to interview staff developers for a story.

- Broaden leadership capacity. Linda Lambert has an excellent book on this subject: *Building Leadership Capacity in Schools* (ASCD, 1998). The great danger is in having leadership reside in one or two people. When these people leave or tire, an excellent program will frequently founder or simply disappear. Forming study groups, establishing mentoring programs, and using problem-based learning and action research with small groups of interested people are all good ways to build leadership capacity.

Situational mastery recognizes that good leadership means there is a fit between the particular talents of an individual or a group and the job to be done. General George S. Patton was an extraordinary tank commander in World War II, but no one would ever have recommended him for a diplomatic position. The principal who is very good in a well-managed, high-achieving suburban school might not be effective in an inner-city school that is failing its students.

Harold Hodgkinson, a leading educational demographer who has had a close look at hundreds of schools, districts, and states, is convinced that "leadership is unpredictable" and that the only training possible is to "train people in what gifts they have for particular settings" (Mark F. Goldberg, *Phi Delta Kappan*, "Demographics—Ignore Them at Your Own Peril: An Interview with Harold Hodgkinson," December 2000, p. 306). This is not a criticism of the many fine leadership programs around the country, but it is recognition of the fact that the qualities of leadership vary from job to job. There is no generic leader or leadership program.

Every educator needs to have a real commitment to social values and to defeating every form of discrimination as a hallmark of her or his leadership. It is simply a fact that we are moving toward a population that will have no dominant majority. More and more, all students are coming into contact with a broader range of ethnic, racial, and religious groups than ever before in our nation's history. If it is not true in a student's K–12 experience, it will be true in the young person's college or vocational training, work life, and travels. We all have a serious stake in making our schools blind to family background, except as we honor that background.

WHAT NEEDS TO BE DONE TO ENSURE A QUALITY TEACHING FORCE IN 2015?

DISCUSSION

The background here is that the U.S. Department of Education's best estimate is that approximately two million new teachers will be needed between 2003 and 2015 to replace the teachers who will retire or leave the profession. Most state education officials and education demographers agree with this figure or something close to it, so there is little question about the opportunity to build a strong teaching force for the first third of the twenty-first century. I placed this question at the end of this book to give the reader some chance to ponder the other questions I posed and to begin to understand the complexity of the education profession.

PERSPECTIVE AND DETAILS

To get at the problems the profession faces, the following issues must be understood: status of teaching as a profession, licensing or certification of teachers, shortages of highly qualified teachers, training of teachers, conditions for teachers. The role of the teacher cannot be overestimated. On the first page of the Consortium for Policy Research in Education and the National Commission on Teaching and America's Future 1998 report, the point is made that teacher expertise is critical in determining student achievement. In fact, the researchers argue, most reforms instituted in schools will succeed or fail in direct relation to the expertise of the teachers implementing them (Darling-Hammond, L. & Ball, D.L., November 1998; "Teaching for High Standards: What Policymakers Need to Know and Be Able to Do," Philadelphia, Pa).

Of course, most of the observations below apply also to school administrators—tens of thousands of whom must be hired and retained in the next twelve years. The overwhelming majority of administrators will come from the ranks of classroom teachers.

Anyone who claims that teachers are not professionals is seriously mistaken. Teachers are certainly professionals who are expected to understand a great deal of content, traditional pedagogy, new and developing methodology and research, relationships with parents and the community, and dozens of other aspects of the teaching profession. You do not fall out of bed one morning able to teach a reluctant student how to read, able to teach level IV French, able to work with a hyperactive or brain-injured youngster, able to teach a group of eleventh graders how to write a substantial narrative or expository essay, or able to construct a short and appropriate problem-based science unit on chemistry for seventh graders. You certainly do not divine how to work with parents, other teachers, and school staff such as psychologists, guidance counselors, and speech therapists. Using what is known about the brain or cooperative learning in the classroom, designing a curriculum unit for eight-year-olds or putting together a serious unit on some recent historical event using primary sources is not something that comes easily to a college graduate without focused training and some practical experience. Designing long-term units in concert with other staff members, often to match new state standards, is a Herculean task for a well-trained, experienced teacher, let alone a new hire.

Millions of students come to school with needs that are difficult to meet. Professional teachers must know reading intervention strategies, must know what math is appropriate at which grade or readiness or age levels, must know how to teach statistics or physics or art or physical education in ways that are effective and will appeal to learners who are not always self motivated. Teachers must have very substantial training in content areas, so substantial that they are actual or virtual majors in those areas. But that is only the beginning.

The teaching profession must be recognized as a real and highly respected profession, not one where people enter it for a few years, learn a great deal about the craft, and then leave for more lucrative or so-called prestigious work. Programs such as Teach for America or the New York City Teaching Fellows program do the nation a great service by getting recent college graduates to work in places where it is difficult to hire teachers—but these people only stay one to three years, just begin to build the skills and learn the technical aspects of the profession that could make them outstanding teachers, and then leave for more lucrative work. They don't build skills over decades, there is no continuity for the school, and they and their colleagues know this is a temporary, if altruistic, endeavor. There is no point including these people in long-term planning for the school. Sadly, these young idealists are not the exception when it comes to people leaving the profession. John Merrow in "Education Week on the Web" writes that "an estimated 30% leave the field within five years; in cities, the exit rate is an astonishing 50 percent" (October 6, 1999).

If you want to require five years of substantial training, perhaps a masters' degree and very high standards for teacher graduates, you will need to provide salary and conditions that will draw people who undergo such training to the profession. Often, schools of education are underfunded and can't do anything like the training a medical or law school can do. Some critics scoff at the role playing in teacher training courses, young adults, for instance, pretending to be five-year-olds who are acting out in some way, and compare that to a rigorous science or English class. It would be better to have some laboratory sessions in the college with real five-years-olds, to have a professional videographer tape the classes and to do careful analysis of what the teacher could have done to manage the class better—but that and every other aspect of teacher training costs money. Teaching young people is an art and a science that must be practiced, analyzed, and reflected upon—no different from considering what went right or wrong in surgery or court.

There is no argument, again, with the notion of strong content training for all teachers, but ultimately these teachers will work with young people who are full of energy and bring all sorts of family, health, learning, and disability problems into the schools. These are not adults who have chosen to attend a class. In a typical fifth-grade class, Mary's parents are going through a divorce, Johnny and Susie are dyslexic and get help from a special education teacher, two other students have severe asthma problems, and three or four others have some difficulty focusing on most lessons for more than eight or nine minutes. The remaining fifteen students present only the "normal" issues when teaching ten-year-olds. The teacher must understand what is going on and have the skills to balance and deal with all of these things while rigorously teaching important content.

Both the quality of the profession and the teacher training programs in the 1,300 schools of education in the country would be helped if teachers could be held to one very high standard nationally. In a July 6, 2001, article in the *New York Times* titled "How to Train—and Retain—Teachers," Vartan Gregorian (former president of Brown University and current president of the Carnegie Corporation of New York) calls for "a national commission to develop standards and national exams for teachers. Such a commission should also be able to develop a model system for measuring teachers' skills and performance."

Voluntary certification from the National Board for Professional Teaching Standards (NBPTS) for experienced teachers already exists and has the backing of the United States Chamber of Commerce, the National Governors' Association, many schools of education, and the nation's two largest teacher organizations—the National Education Association (NEA) and the American Federation of Teachers (AFT). To gain certification from the NBPTS, accomplished teachers with a minimum of three years' experience must complete a series of rigorous, comprehensive tests and present artifacts of classroom work and videotapes of actual teaching, all of which demonstrate their high competence in subject matter as well as their ability to work with children and school staff. Perhaps such a model could be adapted for prospective teachers based on college training, student teaching, and other activities in schools.

Education colleges and the National Council for the Accreditation of Teacher Edcuation (NCATE), the organization that evaluates and gives its imprimatur to colleges of education it deems to have a good program, must raise the ante for what constitutes an adequately trained graduate.

In fact, NCATE has begun this process, and education colleges are now raising such concerns as the value of certain education courses, the nature of student teaching and teaching internships, and the ability of teacher candidates to diagnose student learning difficulties. Candidates for a teaching degree may need to submit a portfolio, including video clips of classroom teaching in a variety of settings, as part of the evidence assuring their qualifications. Accreditation of colleges of education will become more demanding, noneducators may be involved in the process, and the course requirements both in content and methods may become considerably more demanding and realistic.

Teacher salaries and conditions must be addressed very seriously in the next decade if we are to have a well-trained, highly motivated teaching corps. Gordon Ambach of the Council of Chief State School Officers, and a former New York State Commissioner of Education, is quoted in a March 17, 1998, *Christian Science Monitor* article written by Gail Russell Chaddock that "it is very difficult to attract top talent into teaching when salaries are 50 to 75 percent lower than if these candidates go into law or medicine."

John Merrow quotes a former Oakland, California, science teacher, Nancy Caruso, on why she left that district: "I had no water, and I was supposed to teach science. I was toting water from a decaying toilet, basically gallon containers, one at a time, and it was just very frustrating for me. And if you look around, I'm in a decaying building. It's graffiti-ridden, trash everywhere, and it seems like nothing that could get done gets done" ("Education Week on the Web," October 6, 1999).

Bruce Snyder, a very successful teacher in Loudon County, Virginia, left Park View High School where he had been identified as an outstanding mathematics teacher because "Every day you go to work and everything is geared to getting these tests scores up, how we can raise those test scores." No one talked about important or interesting learning or what was good for teachers or students—just the tests. "It was not a healthy environment" (The Washington Post Online, "SOL Tests Create New Dropouts," July 17, 2001).

Anyone can find a few horror stories about education, and no one is suggesting that teachers are demanding salaries on a par with neurosurgeons, but it is true that dozens of inner cities, many rural areas, and some large suburbs are having problems with salaries and conditions that interfere with their hiring a very competent and stable staff. Even at a time when many outstanding young women who years ago would have become teachers now become investment bankers or doctors, at a time when many young people of both sexes who major in anything technical find that it is financial suicide to enter teaching, some of the wealthiest districts in the country still find it fairly easy to recruit candidates, although even they often state privately that the quality of the candidates has diminished in the past twenty years. Teaching often attracts more than the usual number of excellent candidates during an economic contraction, only to lose most of those people when economic conditions improve and teachers see they can earn more under better, and often less stressful, conditions in the private sector.

Much has been written about an impending teacher shortage as we undertake to hire two million or more new teachers in the next twelve years. Pessimists say it can't be done, particularly in the big cities and rural areas where many people do not wish to work. Optimists say that our thirteen hundred schools of education produce enough graduates each year to fill all the vacancies. Realists understand that it is not a question of just filling jobs. The practical questions are the following:

1. Can we find two million qualified and motivated teachers when at least 30 percent of the school of education graduates do not enter teaching?

2. What compromises will many districts have to make to get any candidate—qualified or not—to teach in certain schools or to teach certain subjects? The "Harvard Education Letter: Research Online," July/August 2001, says the teacher shortage "will be felt intensely in high-poverty schools and in certain subjects (math, science, and foreign languages) and programs (bilingual and special education)."

3. What can we do to attract people who will remain in the profession? We are throwing away any chance at continuity of progress or real excellence in places where turnover is 15 to 25 percent per year?

4. How can we attract excellent teachers to poor, rural, and minority areas when the middle and upper-middle class communities pay 15 to 40 percent higher wages?

5. What alternate routes to certification might be available to attract people from other professions or work? How can we guarantee that these candidates have appropriate backgrounds and skills for the certification of their choice? What criteria should be established for alternate routes?

We already have a situation in many parts of this country where emergency and temporary teaching certificates are offered to people lacking in qualification and where the staff turnover is far beyond a healthy point. The question is not whether we can fill two million vacancies, but whether we can fill two million vacancies with well-trained people who intend to make teaching a career.

Salaries are a problem for many teachers. When you talk about a teacher with six or eight years' experience, you are usually talking about someone with at least a masters' degree. Even if you consider that the teacher might coach a sport or supervise a club as well as work in a summer session, in most communities in the United States, it would be difficult to earn more than $35,000 to $40,000 in 2002 for that work in the eighth year of teaching. Compare that to other professionals in their sixth to eighth year with an equivalent education—usually substantial graduate work or a graduate degree.

The American Federation of Teachers (AFT) in a press release dated May 17, 2001 presented its annual state-by-state teacher salary survey for the 1999–2000 school year. "The average teacher salary increase in the 1999–2000 school year was among the smallest in 40 years and failed to keep pace with inflation." The average national salary for teachers was $41,820 for a teacher with 16.1 years of experience. States such as South Dakota, Oklahoma, and Montana paid average salaries ranging from $29,072 to $32,121. The average salary for other white-collar occupations was $77,150 for attorneys; $72,427 for engineers; and $52,323 for accountants, according to the press release.

There are no bonuses or stock options in education. Many corporations pay a greater percentage of their employees' health benefits than many school districts. Young people just do the math or see that their friends in other professions are earning more money and either do not consider teaching or leave after a few years. Many of the brightest, best-educated young people do not even consider teaching as an option.

Conditions are another problem for teachers. In most schools, teachers play little or no role in the governance of the school. Tests and regulations come top down, and many of the brightest, most creative teachers find little to interest them in a system where they "follow orders" for much of their day. Very few teachers have easy access to a telephone or anything resembling an office. They often have no authority to order a book or material for professional growth, and, particularly in cities, the school buildings themselves are not pleasant places in which to work.

There is plenty on the plate, and everything cannot be done at once, but unless there is real openness to seeing teachers as serious professionals and education as a profession worthy of public support and strong funding, in 2016 some pundit will be writing about the dismal conditions in schools and calling for yet another task force to study the problem.

CONCLUSION

Perhaps the best way to conclude this book is with a general question: What else do I need to know about education to feel that I am well informed about enduring issues, recent controversies, and responsible new developments?

Of course, the answer to that would require another book. E. D. Hirsch Jr. once responded to my query about whether there was a significant audience for his cultural literacy ideas that "this is a big country" (Personal Interview, February 8, 1997, Charlottesville, Virginia), and he is without question correct. There are schools in our land that must, or wish to, concern themselves with classroom discipline or Limited English Proficient (LEP) students or a strong honors curriculum or brain-based education or gender equity or race relations or Core Knowledge curriculum or Coalition for Essential Schools policies or Accelerated Schools approaches or any of two dozen other concerns as one of their top three priorities in the next few years. It all depends on local circumstances.

We all want "good" schools and "high-achieving" students, but those words have different meanings to different people. There are schools using cooperative learning, critical thinking, and brain-based education that many people think are very good schools and that produce fine test scores in their states. There are other schools where students wear uniforms, are seated in rows and the instruction is largely direct, and many people think those are very good schools, and they also produce fine test scores in their states—and sometimes these very different schools are in the same state. These descriptions are not an argument for "anything goes." Within the confines of general seriousness of purpose, rigorous instruction, careful attention to the emotional and safety needs of young people, and a powerful desire to help every youngster achieve personal and local goals, there are many roads to success, and no one should be so arrogant as to say, "This is the way and no other."

There were other questions I considered for this book, but time, space, appropriateness, or lack of enough expertise gave me pause. I wanted to include many of the issues that were on the educational front burner, and hope I have achieved that, but I also understood there was no universally accepted list of the top fifteen or twenty issues in education today. Each time I asked a well-informed colleague what questions should be included in a short book, I got a somewhat different response and almost always received one or two questions not previously on my list. If a group of ten educators with many years of experience had done this book, no doubt at least another fifteen questions could have been added—and arguably double that.

"What do I need to know about technology?" was suggested by several people, but I never found a satisfactory way to answer that. Technology changes far too rapidly, and journal articles, conference attendance, and information on the Internet may be the most effective means to keep up with the use of technology in schools. The material in a book should have a shelf life of at least several years from the time it is written to the time it begins to seem less than relevant, and technology information did not meet that criterion. I confess that my limited knowledge of and skills in technology also gave me serious pause.

"What do I need to know about classroom management?" will be a good question for another time. I did write about the issue of safety in this book, but discipline and management have become clouded by changing needs and new approaches.

I worked as development editor on one book on discipline (Richard L. Curwin and Allen N. Mendler, *As Tough As Necessary: Countering Violence, Aggression, and Hostility in Our Schools*, ASCD, 1997),

played a helpful editorial role behind the scenes in the writing of another (Marvin Marshall's *Discipline without Stress, Punishments or Rewards*, Piper Press, 2001), and aided with a new introduction for the
best-selling *Discipline with Dignity* (Curwin and Mendler, ASCD, 1988,
1999). The school landscape today includes charter schools, voucher
programs, magnet schools, gifted academies, private schools, home
schools, religious schools, schools without walls, schools-within-schools,
and several other variations from the shrinking norm—and most of
these schools are subjected to the pressures of increased testing. I need
to visit different types of schools and talk to more people where Richard
Curwin and Allen Mendler's approaches or Marv Marshall's techniques
or William Glasser's work or Alfie's Kohn's or Lee Canter's views or some
other expert's approach is practiced to know the range of what is worthwhile and what the issues are in determining what makes sense in our
changing schools.

"What do we know about the brain, and how does that apply to the
classroom?" is another question I considered. The problems here are
two. First, brain research is still in an early phase. Second, not enough
is yet known about how to use what we know or think we know in the
classroom with any degree of high certainty. In spite of that, I do,
however, fall into the camp that says we should use all that we know,
however tentatively, for classroom support and approaches to learning because, like it or not, the teacher must make decisions about
learning every day. We should base as many of those decisions as possible on the most current and responsible information we have on the
brain, knowing that some of that information is incomplete and still
under partial examination. That is precisely what we do in every other
art or science. I am working right now as the development editor on
a book about the brain and classroom applications. It will be a very
good book; it will also need serious revision in ten or fewer years.
When doctors prescribe medication, they know there will be a better
choice in five or ten or fifty years, but they must do their best today
for a patient—and so must educators.

Second, while many of our current approaches to learning are based
on intuition, incomplete research, and anecdotal evidence, my guess is
that in ten or twenty-five or fifty years when far more is known about
how the brain works, the practices of millions of effective teachers will

turn out to have been brain correct. Most "best practices" are drawn from years of experience and are not likely to turn out wrong-headed. Of course, we will also learn many new, even more effective methods of teaching and ways of learning. Much like my feeling about classroom management, I simply did not feel that I could discuss the question to my own satisfaction, even though I served as the development editor for both of Eric Jensen's ASCD books on the brain and teaching, have read a fair number of articles on the subject, attended conference sessions on the brain and am, as I said earlier, currently working as the develop editor for yet another book on the brain and classroom applications.

Interested readers should look at David Sousa's *How the Brain Learns* (National Association of Secondary School Principals, 1995), Eric Jensen's *Teaching with the Brain in Mind* (ASCD, 1998), and Jensen's latest book, *Arts with the Brain in Mind* (ASCD, 2001).

"What do I need to know about site-based management?" was suggested more than once, but it seemed to me not to be a crucial question at this time, although I certainly will return to this issue in a few years to see what is being written and practiced. In a time when standards and testing dominate the discussion in so many schools and districts, site-based management appears to have receded to a less prominent position than it had seven or eight years ago. Including parents in the life of schools has always been important and continues to be, but that is different from site-based management where several school community constituencies help to determine what will go on in the school. The state standards and tests impose some of the answers—enough that site-based management teams surely have less authority and relevance than they did just a few years ago, and less than was intended by site-based management proponents. For educators interested in this topic, read *Organizing for Successful School-Based Management* (Priscilla Wohlstetter et al., ASCD, 1997).

The general issue of school reform or renewal came up more than once, but that seemed far too broad for a fair question. Virtually any large-minded approach could constitute either broad reform or some substantial degree of renewal. Scheduling, especially block scheduling, was also suggested a few times, but this became a technical issue. Beyond saying that I thought it an excellent idea for secondary schools to consider block scheduling, it was clear to me that a somewhat detailed and technical discussion would have to follow. Robert Lynn Canady and Michael D. Rettig have certainly supplied much of the helpful technical information needed on this subject. Interested readers can consult Robert L. Canady and Michael D. Rettig, *Block Scheduling* (Eye on Education, Inc., 1995).

Some speaker at a conference I attended several years ago insisted that education should work like surgery: find a technique that works and then promulgate that technique to the field. Well, the human body is very consistent from person to person and culture to culture, although certainly unique and emergent complications do crop up in surgery from time to time. The school body is not nearly as consistent. A group of bright, but "poorly behaved" immigrant youngsters may require some different approaches from those applied to a group of equally poorly behaved native speakers. The causes of their poor behavior might be different, their curriculum needs—at least at first for the non-native speakers—will be different, and each student brings an individual culture and set of unique experiences to the classroom.

An unconscious patient in surgery for an inflamed appendix requires similar procedures in any state. A conscious, energetic, bright, healthy nine-year-old in New York City who emigrated two weeks ago from Colombia with his sister and physician mother and computer scientist father may have very different needs from a bright, asthmatic nine-year-old American-Colombian born and residing in New York City who has been in seven schools in the last two years and now lives with his widowed grandmother. With the right education, they could both end up in good circumstances at age eighteen, but it will take more effort and different approaches in behalf of the native youngster in New York City to make this happen.

And that is why our fascinating, infinitely complex profession is filled with questions, more questions, and multiple legitimate answers. And that is why experience, research, rigor, integrity, and flexibility will be the operative words in our profession now and forever.

ABOUT THE AUTHOR

Mark F. Goldberg is an education writer, book development editor, and educational consultant, and speaker. He has edited more than thirty books for the Association for Supervision and Curriculum Development (ASCD) and Corwin Press, Inc., a division of Sage Publications. Dr. Goldberg's previous books are *Lessons from Exceptional School Leaders* (ASCD, 2001), *Profiles of Leadership in Education* (Phi Delta Kappa, 2000), and *How to Design an Advisory System for a Secondary School* (ASCD, 1998). In addition, Goldberg has published more than eighty articles on educational and social issues. Mark Goldberg served in the New York State public education system as a junior high school and high school teacher, curriculum developer, school administrator, and college professor.